BEST
LOSER
WINS

BEST
LOSER
WINS

Why Normal Thinking Never
Wins the Trading Game

Tom Hougaard

HARRIMAN HOUSE LTD

3 Viceroy Court

Bedford Road

Petersfield

Hampshire

GU32 3LJ

GREAT BRITAIN

Tel: +44 (0)1730 233870

Email: enquiries@harriman-house.com

Website: harriman.house

First published in 2022.

Copyright © Tom Hougaard

Paperback ISBN: 978-0-85719-822-8

eBook ISBN: 978-0-85719-823-5

British Library Cataloguing in Publication Data

A CIP catalogue record for this book can be obtained from the British Library.

To the girl at the Bloomberg terminal

CONTENTS

DEAR MARKETS

ROM THE MOMENT I first came across you, I have been fascinated by you. I probably even fell in love with you. I was too young to know what that meant, no more than ten years old. You were featured in a national newspaper – a competition of sorts.

I was too young to play with you, so I observed. Time was not on my side. I was born a few decades too soon to participate in trading like it is possible today. I had to go and live my early life and you went about yours.

When you went through the devastating bear market of 1973, I was just learning to walk. When you roared with anger during the crash of 1987, I was just finishing school. When you took the first steps towards the epic 1990s bull market I was almost ready. But not quite there yet.

So, you sent me a message that would change my life, and I took you up on the invitation, leaving everything behind me to pursue you. I studied you at university, two degrees in fact. I toiled for hours and hours, trying to understand you through the eyes of the conventional economic thinkers, through the eyes of Nobel Prize recipients, and through the eyes of well-meaning journalists and experts.

I wish you could have told me back then not to bother. You are not an equation to be solved. You are far more complex than a model could ever capture. Over and over, you prove yourself to be the elusive mistress that no one every truly understands. You are everywhere and you are nowhere. Universal laws do not apply to you.

My love for you was deep. You gave me so much joy. I gave you my all. You were there when I woke up, and you were there when I went to sleep. You have elevated me when I was fluid, rewarded me beyond my wildest dreams when I was flexible. You have punished me when I was rigid and stubborn, taking all your gifts back – with interest.

And boy did I pursue you. I pursued you like a lovestruck teenager. I approached you from all angles, from Fibonacci ratios to Keltner Channels, to Bollinger Bands, to Trident strategies, as well as mythical vibrations of Gann and Murry Math.

I developed models of the tide swell in the Hudson River to see if you responded to that. I printed out thousands and thousands of charts, applying lines and circles, trying to find a way to dance with you so that my feet didn't get stamped on so much.

I had sore toes, my love. Sometimes my toes were so sore that I had to go to the beach and just throw stones in the water for hours on end, angry that you didn't want to do the tango with me.

You gave me sleepless nights. You gave me tears in my eyes, anger in my body, hurt in my soul, and yet I couldn't let you go. I knew there was more to it, and I knew I had to keep looking.

I gave you everything because you made me feel alive. You gave me a purpose. You gave me challenges so hard even a drill sergeant would have to give you a nod of respect. And I will always love you for it. You kept me on my toes, like a parent wanting only the best for their child.

But you made the lessons obscure. You designed it to look easy. But it was never easy. You made everyone believe that you could be danced with through models, through equations, through indicators, through conventional thinking and through logic. But often there is little logic to you. And I struggled to dance with you for years, until one day by chance you told me your secret. You told me to stop trying to understand you. You told me to understand myself.

I stopped trading. I took the time to understand myself, and I came back. And when I returned to the dance floor, you welcomed me with open arms, smiled, and said, "Welcome back, I see you get it now. Did you bring the band-aids?"

And I did. Best loser wins.

PREFACE

How you feel about failure will to a very large degree define your growth and your life trajectory, in virtually every aspect of your life.

You may want to close this book and think about that for a while. It is quite frightening how deep that sentence is.

What 99% of traders do not realise is that they are looking for answers in the wrong places. Knowledge of technicals, fundamentals, indicators, ratios, patterns and trend lines... well, everyone knows about them – and everyone loses, except the 1%.

What do the 1% do that the 99% is not doing?

What am I doing, enabling me to have the success in trading that I have, which the others are not doing?

The answer is as simple as it is complex. I am an outstanding loser.

The best loser wins.

I have conditioned my mind to lose without anxiety, without loss of mental equilibrium, without emotional attachment, and without fostering feelings of resentment or desire to *get even*.

It is because of how my mind works that I am able to trade in the way that I do. My knowledge of technical analysis is average at best. My knowledge of myself is what sets me apart.

The true measure of your growth as a human being is not what you know, but rather what you do with what you know.

I wrote this book to describe how I transformed myself into the trader I am today, and how I was able to bridge the gap between what I knew I was capable of, and what I actually achieved.

INTRODUCTION

MY NAME IS Tom Hougaard. I am 52 years old. Thirty years ago, I left my native Denmark. I wanted to trade the financial markets and I wanted to do it in London.

I had an idea of what I needed to do to become a trader. I got a BSc in Economics and MSc in Money, Banking and Finance. I thought I had everything I needed to become a trader: the right kind of education; a good work ethic; and passion for the markets.

I was wrong.

On paper, I was qualified to navigate the financial markets. In reality, educational qualifications mean little in the dog-eat-dog world of trading.

This book describes the journey I went through to get to where I am today.

Where am I today?

As I type this, I have not had a losing day in 39 trading days. I run a Telegram trading channel, where my followers witnessed me make £325,000 in the last month alone – in real time, with real-time entries, money management, position sizing, and ultimately the exit of the position. No time delays. No lag. All done before their eyes – time stamped.

This book dispels the myths of what it takes to be a home trader, or any trader for that matter. It has been a journey that saw me initially pursue the path that everyone else takes – a lot of books about a lot of indicators, patterns and ratios – before finally realising that the real answer to the elusive quest for trading profits was right inside of me all along. It truly was the last place I ever thought of looking.

A PROMISING BEGINNING

After completing my university degrees, I started working for JPMorgan Chase. It wasn't a trading job, but it was close enough. Then in 2000 I became a home trader for a year and a half. It only lasted 18 months because I ran out of money.

I had befriended the staff at the broker I traded with. They hired me as a financial analyst. I say *analyst*, but I was a glorified media whore. My mandate was to get the brokerage seen on TV and my *credentials* were an understanding of technical analysis.

I started that job in the summer of 2001. My first customer-facing experience was when the CEO brought me to Royal Ascot – a significant event in the social calendar of the rich and famous. It is a horse racing event, mixed with champagne, funny-looking hats and big cigars.

Only the best and most lucrative clients were invited to this VIP event. On board the executive coach taking the prestigious clients to Ascot, I was introduced as the new financial analyst. "Ask him anything," declared the CEO.

One client asked me what I thought of Marconi. Marconi was a member of the FTSE 100. It had seen better days. It had declined from 1,200 pence to 450 pence over the preceding 12 months.

"Do you think Marconi is cheap?" asked a pharmacist from Luton.

I didn't know it at the time, but my answer – and a similar one on TV a few months later – would eventually get me fired from my job. Even if I had known, I would not have changed my answer:

> Marconi is garbage, gentlemen. Why are you chasing stocks that have fallen in price? The stock market is not like a supermarket, where it makes sense to buy toilet paper when there is a sale on.
>
> Sure, it makes sense to buy toilet paper at a 50% discount, but it makes no sense to buy a stock that has fallen more than 50%. Concepts like 'cheap' and 'expensive' may work in the world of Saturday grocery shopping, but not in the financial markets.

My answer hung in the air like a morbid joke at a funeral. I had barely finished my verdict before I noticed the death stare from my boss. All these clients were long Marconi and they would go on to lose fortunes. Later that year I was on CNBC and I was asked to do a chart analysis of Marconi.

By that point Marconi had fallen to 32 pence – from 1,200 pence. And still people were buying it. I suggested that on the basis of the chart pattern, Marconi would go to zero.

A few newspaper outlets picked up on the story and a few days later I was called to the offices of Sporting Index. The CEO wanted to ask me if it was possible to get these Marconi comments deleted from "that internet".

Marconi went to zero and I was asked to find another job. Fortunately, City Index hired me the same day I left Financial Spreads. I spent seven years on the trading floor at City Index. In 2009 I was made redundant and I have been a private trader ever since.

I have spent the last 12 years of my life perfecting my craft. I am what brokers call a high-stake trader. The average stake size amongst retail traders is about £10 per point risk. I risk anywhere from £100 per point to £3,500 per point.

On volatile days I have traded in excess of £250 million in notional value. I once made a little more than £17,000 in less than seven seconds. One time I lost £29,000 in eight seconds.

That kind of stake size sharpens the senses. Yes, it is a great life when it goes well, but a very challenging one when adversity sets in.

This book describes my journey from an unemployed financial broker in February 2009 to the high-stake trader that I am today. But it is not a conventional trading book.

JUST ANOTHER TRADING BOOK?

The world does not need more trading books. So, I decided not to write one. I know enough about technical analysis to write a few books. I also know that technical analysis does not make you a rich trader. It doesn't even make you a good trader.

I had no ambitions of wanting to write a book, but one day, while I was watching a documentary on YouTube, an advert appeared on my monitor. I recognised the face immediately.

It was a guy who once attended a few speeches I gave on technical analysis, while I was working as a trader at City Index in London. Now he appeared in an advert, promising to reveal the secrets to the financial markets through his courses.

The advert proudly declared that if you wanted to learn to trade like a pro, then this course was what you needed.

As it happened, a friend of mine had attended the course. It took place over a weekend in some plush offices in London. The place was packed and the hopefuls hung on every word of this self-proclaimed guru as he took them through one chart after another.

There was no critical thinking present. No one questioned his claims. Everyone left that office building on Sunday night thinking they would make a small fortune by the coming Friday.

I saw the course notes. It was hundreds of pages of regurgitated material from a standard textbook on technical analysis. There was no original thought behind it. There were no new contributions to the field of technical analysis.

Anyone with half an afternoon at their disposal could find the same material free of charge on the internet. More importantly, my friend told me, the guru never missed an opportunity over the weekend to pitch additional products such as personal mentoring and the advanced course.

THOSE WHO CAN, DO

There is a saying that those who can, do. And those who can't, teach.

I don't agree with that. There are many people who "can" and who also "do". One is not exclusive of the other. Many great "do'ers" see it as part of their life mission to pass on knowledge to those around them. When I worked at City Index, I might not have been an oracle of technical analysis, but I certainly knew more than most of our clients. For that reason I gave technical analysis lessons most evenings to our clients and the many white label clients that City Index had, such as Barclays Bank, Hargreaves Lansdown and TD Waterhouse.

I truly enjoy passing on knowledge and I did the best I could with the knowledge I had. However, what I didn't realise back then was that technical analysis is rather pointless unless it is combined with behavioural response training.

My main beef with the many gurus teaching outrageously expensive weekend courses is their outcome focus. They are driving their agenda by the use of external stimuli, such as portraying themselves in a helicopter or on a private jet, and they portray trading as an easy profession to master, or one where there is a secret to be learned, and once in possession of this coveted secret you become your own ATM. Rarely if EVER will these gurus risk their reputation by disclosing their trades in real time. It is always after the fact. We never hear about their losing trades. This gives the illusion that losing is a mere inconvenience you experience from time to time when trading.

It is only when you sit down in front of the screen on Monday morning, after your overpriced weekend course on trading, and the market is moving in front of you, and you don't have the *after the fact* chart in front of you, that you realise this game is not as easy as the guru told you during the weekend course.

I have written a book that is an antidote to all the rubbish that is being peddled in the trading arena by charlatans who are 99% marketing and 1% trading. They preach their message to unsuspecting people – who sadly believe them – with neither the teacher nor the student realising that they only got 10% of the story.

More importantly, I have written a book which is all about the aspect of trading they never teach you, and how to get to the top of the trading pyramid.

While writing this book, I saw an advert for a technical analysis course in my home country, Denmark. Only the year before, the person running the course had lost 35% of their trading capital on a copy trader account for their followers, before closing the account.

That is the problem with technical analysis. It is very easy to learn, but it should not be touted as the path to untold riches in the financial markets. The gurus appear on adverts suggesting that all you need to make money from the market is to learn technical analysis.

I wish it was that easy, but it isn't.

IF NOT TECHNICAL ANALYSIS, THEN WHAT?

There is a law in Europe that states that brokers offering trading services to retail clients must disclose what percentage of their clients lose money.

I looked up the major players in the industry. According to their websites, around 80% of their clients lose money.

I called one broker to ask how this number was calculated. The number is adjusted quarterly. The broker compares the account balances of its clients from the prior quarter and simply takes the percentage of accounts that have a lower balance than three months earlier.

If the answer to the trading quest was to study technical analysis, then you would not have default rates of 80%. Incidentally, the guru who gave a weekend course to my friend happens to also own a brokerage that he refers all his attendees to. I looked up its default rate.

More than 80%!

So, either his clients are just awful traders, or he is an awful teacher.

I will come to the rescue of both camps and state that to become a profitable trader, you need much more than just technical analysis under your belt.

That is why I wrote this book – to describe the path I have taken to get where I am today. Over the last 20 years I have read many books on technical analysis and trading techniques. I personally find most of them boring and pointless.

All I see in these trading books is one perfect chart example after another. It creates an illusion in the mind of the reader. They absorb these conceited tales, written by traders who espouse the same material as everyone else – material that bears little resemblance to the real trading world. It leaves the reader blindsided to the reality of the trading arena.

Of course, there are exceptions. There are some good books written on techniques and strategies, but most of them are garbage because the author suffers under the illusion that he or she should only show perfect trading examples.

They perpetuate the illusion that trading is an easy endeavour. I think it is fair to say that with a failure rate around 80%, there is absolutely nothing easy about trading.

I dare say that if technical analysis as a subject was comparable to something like dentistry, the vocation would be terminated on account of the 80% failure rate. You don't have a 80% failure rate amongst dentists.

THE MILLION VIEWS YOUTUBE TALK

I was invited by one of the biggest brokers in the world to give a talk about the life of a home trader. They filmed the event, which lasted a few hours. I gave the speech a provocative title:

Normal Does Not Make Money

The broker emailed me last year to say that my video had received five times more views than their second-best video, and that it had now surpassed one million views on YouTube.

This gave me the confidence to push ahead with the book project, because I could see that my message resonated with an audience that wanted to move beyond the conventional teachings in trading.

Although this is not a book about trading techniques, I am not arguing that you can do without technical analysis, or some form of analysis.

There must be some rhyme or reason to your entries and exits, and your stop-loss placement.

However, I am also arguing that techniques alone will not make you rich. Analysis alone will not get you to where you want to be. I imagine you want trading to give you a meaningful side income or perhaps even be your main income.

I am arguing that a normal human being, displaying normal thinking patterns and traits, will never stand a chance of making money trading. In other words, normal won't cut it.

One of the best books ever written on trading is *Reminiscences of a Stock Operator*. There is not a single mention of trading techniques in that book.

Let's face it, we can all learn to walk a tightrope suspended one foot off the ground. However, can you walk across that same tightrope when it is suspended 100 feet off the ground?

In the same vein, we can all trade bravely and aggressively when we are trading one lot, but can you trade with absolute clarity and emotional detachment when you are trading a 10-lot or a 100-lot?

I can't guarantee you will trade 100-lots, but I will describe the process that got me to trade that kind of size.

I am leaving no stone unturned. I have described every facet of life as a trader, from the mundaneness to the excitement, and I have described the exact steps I take every day, week, month and year, to ensure that I am up to the job.

And let me immediately make an important declaration: I am not going to sugar-coat my message. It is an insanely difficult profession, one that is beyond the apparent mental abilities of almost everybody, yet at the same time a profession that will reward you with wealth beyond your imagination, once you understand how this game really should be played.

This book describes how to play the game of trading.

Now you know the end destination. If you don't like the sound of it, now is a good time to put down the book and go to the YouTube and TikTok videos and watch the Ferrari-driving 20-year-old trading coaches tell you how it is all done.

If, however, you want lasting change – not only in your trading, but in how you live your life – then stay with me. Your transformation into a consistent trader will permeate other parts of your life. It will give you a deep understanding of who you are and what you can do to better yourself. The end result is not just more money on your trading account, but a more harmonious and exciting life journey.

LIAR'S POKER

MY JOURNEY AS a trader started when I came across a book called *Liar's Poker*. I was home from school with flu and my dad brought me some books from the library. *Liar's Poker* was one of them.

It is a period piece, written by Michael Lewis, the man behind the book *The Big Short*, which was made into a Hollywood blockbuster.

In *Liar's Poker*, Lewis describes life as a bond trader during the excesses of the 1980s. In his own words it was meant to serve as a warning to future generations about the gluttony of the finance industry, as well as a warning to young people wanting to work in the financial industry.

I think it had the opposite effect. I suspect thousands of young men and women like me read the book and thought to themselves that Wall Street was the place to be.

The book describes a young man travelling from America to Britain to study at a London university and subsequently being hired to work for an American investment bank. It describes what it was like to work on a trading floor and observe some of the big traders there.

I was hooked, and I knew trading would be my vocation. I have since read many other trading books that are perhaps more specific about trading than *Liar's Poker*, but as a starter book, I could not have asked for anything better.

My life changed after reading that book. It was a wake-up call. I went from being a skateboard-loving football fanatic, to being a focused and driven individual. I had found my calling.

I started applying to university degree courses around Europe. I already had a job at a pension fund as an office trainee. After reading the book, I knew that would not be my end destination.

I got accepted to a university in Britain for the following year, but I had a problem. There was no funding. I had to pay my own way. I worked all hours, day and night. During the day I would work at the pension fund, then in the evening I would skate five miles to an amusement park to work there until 1 am.

I absorbed as much information as I could from the Danish finance pages. I would read English books to improve my language skills.

My family was less than supportive. On the big day of departure, I had to make my own way to the airport. They eventually came around and shared my trials and tribulations throughout the years. My sister once told me she chewed her nails the first time she saw me on TV. She was so nervous I would freeze on air.

MY FIRST BIG TRADE

There is a saying in the financial markets that perfectly sums up my first brush with speculation. Don't confuse talent with luck. I was blind to the ways of the financial markets, but I got incredibly lucky.

It was September 1992. I had just been accepted to my university. I had worked hard to earn enough money to finance the tuition fees and living expenses for three years, although I was a little short. I figured I would work through the holidays to make up for the shortfall.

As I was packing up my home and preparing myself to journey to the United Kingdom for my first year as a university student, there was a proverbial hurricane blowing through the currency markets.

The UK was a member of the European Exchange Rate Mechanism (ERM). This was a system introduced by the European Economic Community to reduce exchange rate variability and achieve monetary stability in Europe.

The UK joined the ERM in 1990, but by 1992 the UK was in a recession. The Bank of England found it more and more difficult to honour their commitment to maintain the British pound within a tight band against other currencies in Europe. Speculators were actively betting against the pound, thinking that it was heavily overvalued.

As I was walking to my local bank in Denmark with my savings, looking to exchange my Danish kroner for British pounds, a major drama was unfolding in the financial markets. It was called Black Wednesday.

On 16 September 1992 the British government was forced to withdraw the pound from the ERM after a failed attempt to keep the pound above the lower currency exchange limit mandated by the ERM.

I found the following information about Black Wednesday on Wikipedia. It sets the tone well for what I was about to experience, and what caused a massive windfall for a 22-year-old aspiring trader:

> Soros' Quantum Fund began a massive sell-off of pounds on Tuesday, 15 September 1992. The Exchange Rate Mechanism stated that the Bank of England was required to accept any offers to sell pounds. However, the Bank of England only accepted orders during the trading day. When the markets opened in London the next morning, the Bank of England began their attempt to prop up their currency as per the decision made by Norman Lamont and Robin Leigh-Pemberton, the

then Chancellor of the Exchequer and Governor of the Bank of England respectively.

They began buying orders to the amount of 300 million pounds twice before 8:30 am to little effect. The Bank of England's intervention was ineffective because Soros' Quantum Fund was dumping pounds far faster. The Bank of England continued to buy, and Quantum continued to sell until Lamont told Prime Minister John Major that their pound purchasing was failing to produce results.

At 10:30 am on 16 September, the British government announced a rise in the base interest rate from an already high 10%, to 12% to tempt speculators to buy pounds. Despite this and a promise later the same day to raise base rates again to 15%, dealers kept selling pounds, convinced that the government would not stick with its promise.

By 7:00 that evening, Norman Lamont, then Chancellor, announced Britain would leave the ERM and rates would remain at the new level of 12%; however, on the next day the interest rate was back on 10%.

This was of course all unbeknownst to me, yet it had a material impact on my studies. Had I walked down to the bank just a few days earlier I would have had to pay close to 12 Danish kroner for one pound. By sheer luck I walked straight into, and benefited from, one of the biggest modern-day currency crashes, and I was able to convert my Danish kroner at an exchange rate of about 9 kroner to the pound.

I made an extra £4,000 from my savings. My annual budget with tuition and lodging was £2,500. 'Uncle George' made my university education debt free.

Although the day was called Black Wednesday, many historians argue it was a Golden Wednesday, because the cheaper pound attracted investment. It set the stage for an economic growth spurt in the United Kingdom.

THE PRICE OF A HOTDOG IN PARIS

I wasn't the only one who made a life-changing amount of money that day. George Soros made a billion dollars. It cemented his name as one of the greatest speculators of all time.

And he wasn't the only one who had noticed stark value differences between the European currencies before that fatal day in September 1992. Another trader had too. Actually he wasn't a trader at all. He owned a printing company in East London. We shall call him the Englishman.

When I started working in the City of London, I heard the story of a client who had been holidaying in France. During a visit to Paris, he found himself buying a hotdog at a corner stand, down by the Eiffel Tower.

When it came to pay for the goods, the price for the hotdog was so shocking to our Englishman that he was thinking the hotdog stand owner was trying to cheat him.

He was assured that this was the prevailing price for a hotdog in Paris. He decided to buy another hotdog somewhere else, just to make sure he had not been cheated the first time around. The outcome was the same.

Our Englishman was laying the foundation for one of the greatest single-man bets in the history of the retail trading industry. He walked into a supermarket in Paris and started making a note of the prices for food, drink and other household items.

Back in London our Englishman compared the French prices to the prices for the same goods in his local supermarket, and he concluded that the French franc was hugely overvalued. He called his financial trading house, and spoke to a young broker, who was later to become my boss.

My boss loved to tell the story of how his client managed to turn a £5,000 account deposit into an £8m (that is eight million pounds!) profit. He relentlessly pursued the idea that the French franc was hopelessly overvalued, and he profited hugely from it.

The reason for sharing this anecdote is not merely to tell you a good story, but also to prepare you for what this book is all about. You see, this might have been a great story, had it not been for the fact that the client later went on to lose all of that money, and then some.

Isn't successful trading all about making the money and holding on to it as well?

What 99% of people do not realise is that when you win, there are things happening in your brain chemistry, which – if left unnoticed and unchecked – will have a detrimental effect on your decision making.

ECONOMIC THEORY AND ECONOMIC HISTORY

Studying at university taught me what there was to learn about economic theory. It taught me how the financial markets were put together and how current economic theory tried to make sense of the world around us.

However, it didn't teach me how to trade. It didn't teach me how momentum, psychology and sentiment have a major influence on the financial markets. My degree course did little to prepare me for the real world. I thought that taking a master's degree would change that, and while it was a little more industry relevant, I still felt the market was a big mystery to me.

The idea that you can test variables within an economic system by holding other components constant didn't sit well with me. I am not sure I was consciously mindful of it then, but I saw the world differently.

I didn't think that the markets were efficient. I had a strong belief that the markets were anything but rational. The markets are driven by humans, and if there is something humans are not, it is rational or logical when exposed to stress.

RICH MAN'S PANIC

I enjoyed studying economic history more than I enjoyed studying economic models. One of the pivotal moments came when studying the rich man's panic of 1903 and the panic of 1907. Bernard Baruch, a famed Wall Street speculator, made a substantial amount of money by correctly anticipating the consequences of a failed corner of a railroad stock.

A corner is when a group of people or a syndicate inflates the price of a stock in order to create a buzz, thus trying to entice more gullible investors to join the bandwagon, and then offloads the stock to the latecomers. Today it would be called a pump and dump. Just think GameStop!

What made an impression on me was how Bernard Baruch anticipated the sequence of events. He started to sell short a broad range of popular stocks because he reasoned that the syndicate would have to raise money to keep their ill-fated corner alive. He was right. The general market declined rapidly. The Dow Jones Index fell 49% in a few months, and Baruch profited from it.

From then onwards I found it difficult to study economic models. I found them rigid and too theoretical in concept. I felt they made fallible assumptions. They argued that humans always act rationally.

But mankind most certainly does not always act rationally. As I write this page, I am looking at my quote monitor. The Dow Jones is called down 500 points. The DAX Index is already down 250 points. "Why is that?" I hear you ask. It is because there is a serious virus called coronavirus spreading through the world. Some 80 people have died already.

The market is not so concerned about the 80 people. The market is concerned it is going to get worse. The markets are ALL about perception, sprinkled with economic reality. I don't understand the fundamentals behind a virus, and I don't need to.

My job is NOT to understand the implications of a virus. My job is to understand the players in the market and what they are feeling. They are scared, and I have spotted their fear. So of course I am short. I am not short the market because I think a virus is going to wreak havoc on the global economy. I am short because I think *they think* something terrible is about to happen.

Whatever happens, my job is to read the sentiment and to keep my own emotions in check.

That is essentially what I am going to teach you in this book. I am aligned with reason when it comes to explaining bull markets and bear markets. The health of the underlying economy will drive a market up or down. However, as a day trader I need to have a mental flexibility that is never described or accounted for in economic theory.

I also need to know "when to hold, and when to fold," as Kenny Rodgers sings in 'The Gambler'. Am I a gambler? If I say yes, you might think there is no difference between me and the guy who visits a casino for a bit of excitement.

What if I were to tell you that I make more money than the average professional football player, and I do so not because I am gifted with special abilities to read the markets, but because I have learned to control my emotions?

I am not an unemotional sociopath. I feel. I love. I cry. I ache. I mourn. I laugh. I smile. You can be a nice guy and still finish on top. But you do need to learn to think differently than the 99% does, when you are trading. We will get to that soon enough.

JPMORGAN CHASE

After my graduation I interviewed for many graduate jobs within the banking and finance industry. I didn't get my dream job, working as a trainee trader, but I did get a good job working for Chase Manhattan Bank, later called JPMorgan Chase.

It was an invaluable experience. I arrived with a bagful of enthusiasm. Working for an American investment bank was probably the best thing that could have happened to me.

I was able to channel my enthusiasm for the financial markets into my work. I worked with portfolio analysis and performance benchmarking, which meant I was able to observe the financial markets unfold before my eyes every single day.

I happened to sit right next to a Bloomberg terminal. I loved that machine. I would often sneak into the office building on Saturdays and Sundays to devour analysis and trading stories, and download data.

The great thing about working for an American bank is that there is a very different work ethic to typical European companies. This may have changed in the last 20 years, but when I was working at JPMorgan we were literally allowed to work as many hours of overtime as we wanted.

I worked for JPM for close to three years, and in those three years I never had a month where I didn't do at least 40 hours' overtime. You got used to working long hours with focus because the job required forensic attention to detail.

By the time I left the bank, I was a hardened and seasoned workaholic. I don't say that with pride, but I don't think there is any point in hiding the fact that the reason for my success was not due to immense intelligence, but rather my work ethic. I just worked longer hours than the others. I made the sacrifice for what I wanted.

My attitude reminds me of the ethos of Navy Seals, the American special forces unit: anything in life worth doing is worth overdoing. Moderation is for cowards.

My dream finally did come true, when I walked onto a trading floor for the first time.

THE TRADING FLOOR

WALKING ONTO A trading floor is a special experience. I vividly remember being interviewed for a trading job after my university graduation. This took place on the trading floor of Handelsbanken, the Scandinavian bank, and the guy who interviewed me was the head of trading.

I could tell that he was intensely focused on something else, and I was an inconvenient distraction. I have been in that situation many times in my trading life. Having a big position on in the market and then having to deal with the trivialities of the world outside of trading can be a peculiar experience.

Boxing Day 2018 is a great example. I was trading the biggest one-day rally in the history of the Dow Jones Index, while eating Christmas pudding. I had to hide my mobile phones under the dinner table so as not to offend my host, and I had to fake numerous trips to the toilet so I could watch the chart on one phone and the broker platform on another.

I arrived at the trading floor of Financial Spreads with a very different attitude to most of my colleagues. As I know many of them will read this book, I owe it to them to explain that I am not accusing them of being lazy. I had lots to learn, including the fact that when the markets are quiet, there really isn't much for brokers to do.

What I found was that people would sit around and read the newspapers or comic books. If the phone didn't ring, you could hardly force a broker to do anything. I think this was the biggest culture shock I experienced – the contrast between a normal office job and a trading floor.

Working on a trading floor is intimidating at first. As the months go by, you become immune to the money changing hands. It is all just numbers on a screen. I once walked in at 6 am to find that a Russian client was on a margin call for $10m. I quickly calculated that it would take me 133 years on my current salary to make $10m. By 7 am he had wired the funds over. This was a private trader. I was in awe. Inspired.

There is a unique atmosphere present on a trading floor. When it is busy, it is nothing short of a gigantic melting pot of human emotions. I once saw a colleague of mine kick his PC so hard – repeatedly – that IT engineers had to come and replace it.

It is hard to fathom that the financial markets are a complex mechanism if you just look at what is happening on a trading floor. It reminds you more of a local market stall on a busy Saturday morning in any given town anywhere in the world, where one stall owner is trying to out-voice the next.

When you witness the raw, uncensored emotions that unfold before your eyes on the trading floor, it is difficult to see how that fits into a finely tuned global economic environment that makes up the very fabric of our modern society and civilisation.

Impulse buying, panic selling, holding on to losses, refusing to admit defeat, greed, stupidity, stubbornness, despair, tears, abject depression, exhilaration and excitement are all on display here, and all in quick succession of each other.

I worked for Financial Spreads for a year, and was then asked to leave. The same day I was headhunted to City Index, which was owned by ICAP – the biggest US government bond broker in the world.

City Index had about 25,000 clients, of which 3,000 were active most days. These clients would trade currencies, commodities, stock indices, individual stocks, options, bonds and anything in between. I must have witnessed tens of millions of trades in my career, executed by thousands of people. Very few, if any, of them stood out, and if they stood out it was for all the wrong reasons. For every success story, I can tell you ten horror stories.

NO MEMORY OF THE GREAT TRADERS

I recently spoke to a friend of mine, who is the CEO of a trading company in London. I asked him if there were traders who had stood out during his 30 years working on trading floors. He said that over the years he had witnessed many bizarre things, but in terms of good traders, he had seen very few.

Here is a man who has spent his entire adult life on trading floors, yet he is incapable of remembering people who did well. We are talking about a percentage of successful traders so infinitesimally small that it makes you wonder why anyone would want to trade in the first place, or if anyone could ever get good at this profession. The conversation with him went as follows.

Tom: You have worked in the contract for difference (CFD) industry for 30 years. You must have seen some good traders along the way. Can you tell me about them?

CEO: I wish I could. I have seen many people make a lot of money, but very few managed to keep the money. I started in the industry at a time when CFD trading was not a mainstream tool. It was mostly very wealthy people or people who worked in the industry that had CFD accounts. These clients back then often traded as part of an old boys' club kind of network. It meant they mostly traded specific shares and some commodities. Back then trading was nowhere near as prolific as it is today.

Tom: Were they good traders?

CEO: No, I would not say they were. We had clients who were well-known personalities in the City, and their personal trading was often atrocious, even though they were hedge fund traders or fund managers. It was almost as if they lost their discipline when trading their own money. I am certain they would not be allowed to trade for their clients in the manner they traded for themselves.

Today we have far more smaller traders, but the pattern is remarkably similar between a small trader and a large trader. Almost all clients have more winning trades than losing trades. As such you could argue that they are good traders.

However, they tend to lose more, much more, on their losing trades than they win on their winning trades. The ratio is that for every pound they win, they lose about £1.66.

Tom: How does a CFD broker make money out of that?

CEO: Well, believe it or not, we want our clients to win. I have a network of contacts in the CFD industry. I regularly meet with CEOs of competing companies. Although we are competitors, and we would do anything to outmanoeuvre a competitor, we do have one shared wish. We wish our clients would trade better.

We try our best to help them. We give them every tool under the sun. We give them favourable spreads, and we give them news services. We give them sophisticated charting packages. We give them data. We give them analytical tools to measure their performance.

In short, we do absolutely everything we can to ensure they have all the tools they need to make money. And then we let them trade. The problem is that most smaller accounts tend to lose within a short space of time.

Trust me when I say I wish it was different. I don't know what more we as brokers can do for our clients. We prefer clients to make money because there is clear evidence that those who trade and win, carry on trading. That is better for business.

The truth of the matter is that you can clearly see the difference between a consistently profitable trader and a normal trader. Their approach is very different.

Tom: How can you tell whether someone knows what they are doing?

CEO: There are a multitude of parameters that we may look at. If I have to narrow it down to the five most important factors, it would be these:

1. Account size.
2. Trade frequency.
3. Ratio of time spent holding winning trades versus losing trades.
4. Adding to winning or adding to losing trades.
5. Trading with a stop-loss.

Someone who opens an account with anything less than £100 will, with a very high degree of certainty, lose that money, sadly. Someone who trades everything and anything, i.e., overtrading, will eventually lose their money.

Anyone who is unable to hold on to their winners, but holds on to their losing trades, will eventually lose their money.

Anyone who adds to their winning trades will catch our attention (positively), but anyone adding to their losing trades will, with near certainty, lose their account deposit at some point.

Anyone trading without a stop-loss will follow that path too. We sadly see it all the time.

> As you can see, as brokers we do everything we can to help people make money, but people are people, which means they will find a way to self-sabotage.

CONDITIONS 20 YEARS AGO

I keep an eye on all brokers, to make sure I trade with the best and cheapest. Why would I pay 1.5 in spread if I can pay 1 in spread? That is simple economics. I run a business, and I want to spend as little on transaction costs as possible.

One of my favourite instruments to trade is the German DAX Index. Today when I trade, I pay a 0.9 point spread in the DAX.

However, when I started trading some 20 years ago, the spread intraday in the DAX was 6 to 8 points. I remember vividly trading the Dow intraday. You had to pay an 8-point spread in the Dow for the intraday product.

If you wanted to trade the quarterly contract the spread was 16 points. This was at a time when the Dow was trading around 10,000. Today I am trading the Dow with a 1-point spread and the Dow is now trading around 35,000.

You are much better off trading in 2020 than you were trading in 1999. It was much harder to make money trading back then. The market has to move significantly less in your favour before you are at breakeven now, compared to 1999.

Another major advantage that people who start trading today have is the tools available from the brokers. Look at virtually any trading platform today, and you will see the length brokers go to in order to help you make money.

You have access to hundreds of technical studies. You have access to instant news flow. You have the option to be trained through online material and webinars. You have access to Level 2 data for stocks all over the world.

You have decent bid-ask spreads. If an institutional trader from 30 years ago saw the tools that you are trading with today, he or she would be green with envy.

You have at your disposal every single conceivable analytical tool available from the vast resource pool of technical indicators. You have Bollinger Bands, you have Keltner Channels, you have moving averages. You have tools that I have never even heard of or used myself.

Suffice it to say, every broker in the world has spared no expense in their effort to provide you with every opportunity to make as much money as you possibly can out of the markets.

But it matters nothing. Most people will fail. The failure rate is astronomical in the trading industry. No one is immune to statistics.

NORMAL IS A LOSER

There is something inherently wrong with the approach of people who are trading. We have to assume that most people in society are normal, well-adjusted human beings. Their pattern of behaviour, while leaving room for personality, is most likely very similar.

From cradle to grave, from morning to night, from one year to the next, the average person is engaged in a remarkably similar pattern: pattern of thought, pattern of action, pattern of hopes and dreams, fears and insecurities. We call that person *normal*.

If normal is the familiar pattern, and if normal is opening an account with a CFD broker and proceeding to lose the money (sooner or later), then normal is simply a representative of everyone else. Everyone who is normal will end up losing.

Is that a push too far? Let us look at the evidence. Let us take a look at the norm for a typical CFD trader in the retail trading space.

Even though your broker makes all the tools under the sun available to you, no one is immune to the statistics of the financial markets. Unless you have gone through some sort of structured training, or you have been schooled by someone who is walking the path you yourself want to walk, or you give this endeavour some serious thought, you will most likely fail in the financial markets.

Look at any broker website in the European Union, and you will see the failure rate. Brokers are obliged by law to post this on the front page of their website. Here are some of the biggest and most well-known CFD brokers in the world, and their failure rates:

BROKER	FAILURE RATE
IG Markets	75%
Markets.com	89%
CMC Markets	75%
Saxo Bank	74%
FX PRO	77%

Rates correct as of 7 November 2019.

I know you like to think you are different. However, in the eyes of the financial markets, you are statistically like everyone else.

You can look at the top ten brokers of the world and the statistics do not change. You can look at CMC Markets, you can look at IG Markets, you can look at Gain Capital, or you can look at any one of the top tier or second tier CFD brokers. No one will have a failure rate less than 70%.

NORMAL IS NOT GOOD ENOUGH

Tools do not make you a top trader. Techniques do not make you a top trader. If you want to be a good trader, if you want to achieve the level of success that you know is possible, you immediately need to stop thinking that the path to riches in trading has anything to do with the tools or techniques you are using.

Yes, of course you need a strategy. Yes, you need a plan. Yes, you need to understand the markets. So, what is this book all about, if it is not about tools and strategies?

Well, let me address that question from a different perspective. Let me address it from the perspective of the people who work in the industry as brokers and sales traders and as marketing people.

Do they trade?

I would say it is likely they do not. Yet, traders are taking advice, guidance and training from them; they being guided by people who are no better at trading than they are.

It reminds me of Fred Schwed's book, *Where Are the Customers' Yachts?*, in which he says that Wall Street is the only place in the world where people who arrive to work by train and bus give advice to people who arrive by limousine and helicopter (slightly paraphrased for a more modern touch). Traders are being guided by people who can't trade!

WRONG FOCUS

When you go to trading shows, read trading magazines or look at the online education materials on broker websites, 100% of the focus is on what I call *How To*:

- How do I scalp?

- How do I swing trade?

- How do I day trade?

- How do I trend follow?

- How do I trade the foreign exchange (FX) market?

- How do I use Ichimoku charts?

- How do I trade with moving average convergence divergence (MACD) or stochastics?

This is perfectly normal. The trade shows and magazines are geared towards providing the solutions that most people believe they need in order to make money in the financial markets. The brokers are following the same path. They provide the information that they think traders need and that traders think they need.

Newcomers to the industry of trading are often guided by the very people who are likely to set them off on the wrong path. They are led to believe that it is all about technique and strategy – no one is preparing them for the fact that it isn't strategy that will set them apart from other traders.

It is how traders think about their strategy – and their ability to follow the strategy – that will set them apart.

Do you not wonder if this is the right path for you? Do you not wonder about the futility of dedicating all your resources to one pursuit, when virtually everyone who walked that path before you has failed?

You should. You really should ask yourself what makes you different to the 90% of traders that do not make money. If you are normal – as in you do what everyone else is doing – then you won't make it.

NORMAL WON'T CUT IT

The organisers of one of these trade shows invited me to give a talk. This show was in London, and I was told I could talk about whatever I wanted. I decided to give a talk about the disastrous failure rate in the trading industry.

My argument is that if 90% of all CFD accounts lose money, the problem is a human problem. I feel I am making a reasonable assumption when I say that everyone opening a CFD account is a normal person with a normal way of thinking. There must be something inherently wrong in the way normal people think and act that makes trading so unsuccessful for them.

IT SHOULD BE EASIER THAN EVER TO MAKE MONEY TRADING

I mentioned previously how small today's bid-ask spreads are compared to 20 years ago. Therefore, it should be easier than ever for traders to make money. However, it isn't.

People are still struggling to make money trading. My main premise of this book is to get to the bottom of this conundrum. The approach I have taken is centred around the following facts:

1. It has never been easier to trade. The IT infrastructure is superb for traders.

2. The spreads have never been lower.

3. The margins have never been more favourable.

4. The tools have never been so readily available.

5. The brokers have never done as much for their clients as they do now.

6. The stock indices have never been higher, meaning there is volatility.

To reiterate, I assume that people who open trading accounts are normal, well-adjusted human beings – without using this as a slight or an insult – who are perfectly capable of functioning within society.

The questions I want to ask, and answer, are these: what does normal behaviour look like? How can I avoid being normal when I trade? If we assume that 80–90% of people trading are normal people, I want to avoid acting like they do.

ARE YOU NORMAL?

My argument, provocative as it is, asks an essential question: are you thinking like everyone else is thinking and approaching trading like everyone else is approaching trading?

If so, you will have a problem.

If you think like everyone else, is it so strange that you get the results that everyone else gets?

Let us take a look at what normal behaviour is.

Normal behaviour is to engage in a never-ending cycle of education, looking for the next new edge. I knew from the moment I read *Liar's Poker* that I wanted to be a trader, but I never had any formal training in how a good trader behaves. Why should I? I was always told that a good trader buys low and sells high. But every time I bought low, it always went lower and lower. So what kind of advice was that?

And yet this is the advice we listen to when we start. This is the benchmark, and if this is the benchmark, then it is a miracle that it is only 90% that are losing. It should be 100%, because buying low and selling high is a sure recipe for ruin.

People will attend weekend courses hoping to learn secrets. People will study and learn to use tools such as candlestick analysis, stochastics, Relative Strength Index (RSI), MACD and moving averages. The list goes on and on. All of this is normal behaviour in a nutshell.

EVEN THE BIBLE IS WRONG

Even the bible of technical analysis doesn't do much to help a person on their way, once the initial learning curve is over.

The bible of technical analysis was authored by Robert D. Edwards and John Magee. The book is called *Technical Analysis of Stock Trends*, and it has sold millions of copies since its first printing in 1948.

What most readers don't realise, however, is that Edwards and Magee were not the real creators of modern technical analysis. Rather, it was a little-known technical analyst named Richard W. Schabacker.

A brilliant market technician, Schabacker codified almost everything there was to know about technical analysis up to his time – which included such pioneering work as the Dow theory of Charles Dow.

Between 1930 and 1937, Schabacker taught several courses to serious Wall Street traders and investors. Unfortunately, he died in 1938 when he was not even 40 years old.

Shortly before his death, Schabacker gave a mimeographed copy of his lessons to his brother-in-law, Robert D. Edwards, who rewrote Schabacker's lessons with the help of his collaborator, John F. Magee, an MIT-trained engineer.

As a result, it was not Schabacker who received credit for the original compilation of technical analysis, but Edwards and Magee, whose work became a perennial bestseller.

Let me be clear: reading a book like *Technical Analysis of Stock Trends* is a must, but please don't think that it will make you a professional, profitable trader, any more than reading a manual on tennis will enable you to compete with Rafa Nadal.

I see newcomers make classic mistakes after reading books on technical analysis. They will study indicators such as RSI and stochastics, and they will excitedly declare that a market is 'overbought' or 'oversold'.

What they don't realise is that 'overbought' is an emotional expression for a psychological conceptualisation of 'expensive'. The people reading a stochastics chart are led to believe – through a mathematical manipulation of data – that the market is now expensive, and it should be shorted.

The same can be said for 'oversold'. It is another way for the mind to tell you that the market is cheap, and that there is value associated with it.

I'll give you an example. Yesterday was a particularly bearish day in the Dow Jones Index and the German DAX 40 Index. I was short all day and I had one of my better days, all verified and documented on my Telegram channel. It was 1 October 2019.

Towards the end of the day, when the Dow Index was falling even lower, a student of mine contacted me and asked me a very alarming question. The conversation was in Danish, and I have translated it here.

"Tom, have you seen the stochastics indicator? It is deeply in 'oversold' territory. Do you think it is a good idea to buy now, ahead of the close?"

I reply: "Hmm, I am short… maybe you should ask someone else."

He goes on to express his absolute shock that I am short, and a little later he goes on to state that he has bought the Dow at 25,590.

Of course, when there is a buyer, there is a seller. However, I am not convinced that buying the Dow Jones Index ten minutes before the close, on a day where it has fallen 400 points, is a good idea.

It reminds me of the kind of thinking I would have done 20 years ago. Not today though. If I buy the Dow on a weak day, just before the close, it is to close a short position. I value my sleep too much to carry a position overnight.

I said to him: "You had all day to find a short entry. What are you hoping to achieve by being a buyer now? Are you thinking that because it has fallen 400 points, now it is cheap, and maybe just before the close, you may see some buying of these cheap stocks?"

I used to think like that too. That was when I was *not* profitable.

The Dow didn't rally into the close. There was no bounce. I am sure my student didn't lose a lot. It wasn't so much his wallet I was concerned about – it was his way of thinking.

That is what this book is about. It is about making you think the right way about the market. That is where the 80–90% of losing traders tend to go wrong.

CLOSE THE SCHOOL

If trading was a school, it would be closed. No school or university could function if 90% of its students failed their exams.

We are all pretty much normal people. We fit in and function well within the fabric of modern society. If every person engaged in trading is a normal human being – and I assume they are, meaning they are well-functioning, intelligent, considerate, hard-working – then why is there a 90% failure rate in our industry?

That doesn't make any sense at all. Usually when people work hard at something they will succeed, or they will see some degree of success. That doesn't appear to be the case with trading. Other professions do not have a 90% failure rate.

If you go to the dentist, and you are told there is a 90% chance he will not be able to fix your teeth, you are out of there like a shot. Yet, those are the odds that face a private trader. But it doesn't have to be like that.

As traders, we tend to engage in a never-ending, predictable cycle. We trade well for a while. We are happy. Our discipline weakens. We lose money. We strengthen our resolve, and we get more education. We do well for a while. We lose money. We stop – sometimes for a while, sometimes permanently.

Sound familiar?

The sad part about this cycle is that everybody has good spells in trading. Everybody has periods when they make money. Everybody has their moments. I am sure you have too.

So what happens? What happens is that 99% of people do not know how to lose. The emotions they experience when they lose cause them to act in a manner which is not in their own best interest.

Emotions are response driven. Say you hear a funny joke, and you laugh out loud. That is an emotion. When you hear the joke the next time, you don't laugh. Your mind has become habituated to the joke.

When you fall in love with a beautiful man or woman you experience strong emotions, and your inner life is in beautiful turmoil. When you see that person, you just want to express your love for him or her, and be united with them, gaze into their eyes.

As time goes by, your loving turmoil is replaced with a sense of calm. You love being around them, but the feelings of passion are less pronounced than they were in the beginning. You have become habituated to the other person.

A free solo climber, climbing intimidating rock surfaces without ropes, is faced with severe consequences if they lose their grip. They acclimatise their minds through years of practice, so that their amygdala – the emotional response centre of the mind – is not firing on all cylinders when they are climbing. They are calm.'

An elite solider is scared to death the first time he is in a combat situation. That is why his first combat situation will be a simulation. And the next one. And the next one. And little by little, his fear is trained out of him, through the use of repetition, breathing awareness and habituation.

For every hour you spend on technical analysis, you must set aside at least 25% of that time for what I call internal analysis. You need to know what your weaknesses are. You need to know what your strengths are. You need to know what you are good at, and you need to know what you are not good at.

If you don't spend time trying to improve these things, how will you get better? Very few people, if any, will engage in that level of introspection in order to gain the results they want. If making money trading is your goal, and 99% of people lose, and 99% of people think analysis and strategies are the key to trading profits, you can be 100% sure that strategies and analysis are not the key to trading profits.

43 MILLION TRADES ANALYSED

There is a piece of research that makes for very interesting reading. It was the brainchild of an analyst called David Rodriguez, and it is brilliant. Rodriguez worked for a major FX broker, and he attempted to find out why there was such a high failure rate amongst its clients trading currencies. The broker had some 25,000 people who traded FX daily.

Rodriguez investigated all the trades executed over a 15-month period. The number of trades was truly staggering. The 25,000 people executed close to 43 million trades. From a statistical point of view, that created a statistically significant and immensely interesting sample space to investigate.

Specifically, Rodriguez and his colleagues looked at the number of winning trades. I would like to give you an opportunity now to think about how many trades were winning trades and how many trades were losing trades. You can represent it as a percentage of the overall 43 million trades.

If you feel it has any influence on the answer you want to give, I can tell you that most of the trades were executed in Euro Dollar, Sterling Dollar, Dollar Swiss and Dollar Yen.

However, the vast majority of the trades were executed in Euro Dollar, where the spread is very tight. Unfortunately, that doesn't seem to make much of a difference to the outcome.

62% of all the trades by the broker's clients ended in a profit. That is a little more than six out of ten trades. That's a good hit rate. A trader with a hit rate of six out of ten should be able to make money from trading.

Of course, it does depend greatly on how much he wins when he wins and how much he loses when he loses. Therein lies the problem for the 25,000 people.

They were very successful in terms of hit rate. Yet when you look at how much they made on average per trade and how much they lost on average per trade, you soon realise that they had a major problem. When they won, they made about 43 pips. When they lost, they lost about 78 pips.

There's nothing wrong with having a system where you lose more on your losing trades than you win on your winning trades. However, it does require that you have a sufficiently high hit rate in order to absorb the losing trades.

A colleague of mine, a professional trader from South Africa who trades at a hedge fund, has a hit rate of about 25%. I tell his story in greater detail later in the book, but let me explain the term *hit rate* in the context of his hedge fund.

When his hedge fund loses on a trade, they lose 1X. When they win, they win as high as 25X. It stands to reason that my friend is immensely profitable even though he doesn't have a convincing hit rate, at least not from a traditional perspective.

What I find particularly interesting is how much bad advice there is in the trading industry. You will often hear traders talk about risk-to-reward ratio, which in itself is fairly innocent, unless the trader takes it literally and applies it on a trade-by-trade basis.

When I call out trades in my live TraderTom Telegram group, I will always announce a stop-loss. Always! However, I often get asked if I have a target in mind. The answer is quite often a little sarcastic: "No, my crystal ball is out for repairs," or if I am particularly grumpy and tired, I will be rude and say, "Sorry amigo, but do I look like a fortune teller to you?"

Yes, I know – that isn't very polite. I'm sorry. Ignoring my blatant inability to be polite when I am faced with the same question for the 450th time, there is a deeper meaning to me not calling targets on my trades. It has a lot to do with risk versus reward.

RISK VERSUS REWARD

I personally find the whole risk-to-reward concept enormously flawed, but since I am the only one who ever talks about it, I accept that I am probably wrong. Still, hear me out.

How on earth do I know what my reward will be? I literally do not know. Even if I pretended to know – say, by using a measured move calculation or a Fibonacci extension – I know myself well enough to know that I will have added to my trade along the way. When it got to my target, I would not close it, because that is my philosophy.

I would kick myself if I closed a trade at my target, and then it went even further. I would rather give away some of my open profits than miss out on potentially even more profits.

Now I am probably making a big fuss out of nothing, but targets are not for me. I want to see what the market will give me. I am prepared to accept that this may mean I will give away some of my open profits. I have lost count of the number of times I have had a 100-point winner in the Dow, which then turned into a zero.

A week before writing this (all documented of course) I had one such winner, which turned into a big fat zero. Some less-than-happy traders confronted me in my live trading room as to why I had not taken my profits. It is difficult to explain, but it is all to do with pain.

It gives me much less pain to kiss a 100-point winner goodbye than it does to take my 100 points, only to see the market moving even more in my favour.

It is because of this philosophy that I am at times able to make 400–500-point gains, as I did today. It is one or the other. I don't think you can have the best of both worlds!

INTERVIEW WITH CNN

In an interview with CNN some years ago, I was asked about the traits of winning traders. In this very candid interview, I highlighted a few points that I felt differentiated the winning traders from the losing traders. It was based upon my experiences from observing millions of trades by retail traders, while I was on the brokerage trading floor. Here are the main differences I identified:

1. TRYING TO FIND THE LOW

When the market is trending lower, whether intraday or over a longer time frame, there seems to be a tendency for retail traders to attempt to find the low of the move.

Whether that is out of a desire to buy cheap, or because they use ineffective tools, I simply don't know. What I do know is that this trait is immensely damaging to anyone's trading account.

Winning traders seem to be much more trusting of the prevailing trend. This attitude adjustment may seem trivial, but it literally makes the difference between the winning trader and the losing trader.

Over time the losing trader will repeat his distrust in the prevailing trend and will take positions against it. He will do so because from an emotional standpoint it appears as if he is buying a market that is cheap or selling short a market that is expensive.

This is emotionally satisfying, like buying toilet paper at a 50% discount from the local supermarket, but the financial markets are not supermarkets. There is no 'cheap'. There is no 'expensive'. There is just the prevailing price.

The winning trader, however, is not emotionally attached to an idea of 'cheap' or 'expensive'. He is focused on this moment right now, and in this moment right now the market is trending, and he trusts this trend and can unemotionally join this trend without internal discomfort.

2. TRYING TO FIND THE HIGH

The opposite also holds true. When the market is trending higher, traders tend to want to find a place to sell short. Although it must be said that people are generally better at jumping on board a market that has already risen than they are at jumping on board with a short position in a market that has already fallen significantly.

If the market has moved higher by a significant amount, especially in the very short term, retail traders tend to want to fade the rising prices, i.e., they look to establish short positions. Again, this is probably the result of a distorted view of things being cheap and things being expensive.

3. THINKING EVERY SMALL COUNTER-MOVE AGAINST A TREND IS THE START OF A NEW TREND

I have sat on a trading floor through the darkest days of the financial markets. For example, 15 September 2008, when Lehman Brothers was declared bankrupt, the Dow Jones Index fell 4.5%.

Throughout that trading day, there were two attempts to rally. Both failed. It was tragic to see how many clients tried to buy the low of the day, only to see the Dow move lower and lower.

Whenever there was a single green candle on the 5-minute chart that day, we saw the buy order flow into our position monitors on the trading floor. It seemed as if the clients were possessed by the notion that a low was near, and that they had to be the one buying it.

The low didn't come that day. Nor the next day.

This is a common trait amongst traders. They think that every single little counter reaction against the trend is the beginning of a new trend. More fortunes have been lost trying to catch the lows in a falling market than in all wars put together (okay, this is an unsubstantiated statement made for emphasis, but please don't attempt to catch lows).

It seems obvious to me that newcomers and probably also some seasoned traders – profitable or unprofitable – believe that successful trading is all about charts.

This belief is a detriment to their accounts, because no one ever took the time to tell them otherwise. No one told them, or thought to tell them, or knew enough to tell them, that actually focusing all your time on your charts is a mistaken strategy. We'll look at this further in the next chapter.

EVERYONE IS A CHART EXPERT

I ONCE DECLARED IN an article that you can learn the basics of technical analysis over a weekend. I may have exaggerated a little – but only a little.

I know without an inkling of doubt that a chart expert does not equate to a trading expert. I have seen so many of my trading friends build impressive libraries of technical indicators and acquire knowledge about both known and obscure technical indicators. But it didn't translate into making more money. When it comes to charts, less can be more.

Charts can be as simple or as complicated as you want. There seems to be a tendency amongst traders to make charting more complicated than it really needs to be. I have seen many new traders plaster their charts with so many tools that they can barely see the price chart itself.

It surprises many people, especially newcomers, when they see my chart screens. There is not a single indicator on them. Not a single one. I might be old fashioned, but I don't need these extra tools.

My job as a trader is to find low-risk trading setups. My approach to trading is not centred around any other tool than price itself. All indicators – more or less – are built from time and price. Therefore, the indicator is a distortion of the reality I am seeing right in front of me.

The markets can be range bound, or the markets can trend. Some indicators work well in ranging markets. These usually perform terribly in trending markets. Other indicators work well in trending markets, but are dreadful to use in range-bound markets.

As a famous trader friend of mine, Tepid2, once said on the now-defunct trader feed Avid Trader: "Indicators – they all work some of the time, but none of them work all of the time."

I think that many of the 90% of people that lose money trading may very well have excellent chart reading abilities. They can read charts very well, and they understand patterns too.

However, I happen to think there is much more to trading than knowing a head and shoulder formation, a bar chart pattern or a Fibonacci ratio.

I have seen outstanding traders juggle millions of pounds worth of stock index futures contracts using nothing but a simple ten-minute chart. In fact, I do that myself every single trading day.

I truly believe that what separates the 1% from the 99% is how they *think* when they are in a trade, how they handle their emotions when they trade. That is not to say that there is no merit to learning the craft of chart reading. I know from my own experience that chart reading is an absolute must for my decision making, but that is only a small part of the whole trading picture.

The proliferation of gurus selling trading courses is evidence there is a demand to learn the art and craft of trading. I suspect the 'shortcut' of a weekend course is a much more appealing proposition than spending that time reading books.

If a guru holding a weekend course on trading claims that you will be qualified to trade "like the millionaire professionals" by the Sunday night, then the unsuspecting will select that option. It is perfectly natural to expect a human being to drift down the path of least resistance.

Learning any new skill takes time. So when you see an advert saying "learn a new language in 30 days", you might not believe it consciously, but subconsciously you want to believe it, because people love shortcuts. Similarly, a diet book that promises you will lose 5kg in a year is unlikely to sell as well as one promising you will lose 5kg in two weeks.

My philosophy to life is different from so many other people's. This is the reason I have what so many people dream of. I will choose the path of most resistance, because I know I need to stay clear of the opinion of the 99%.

If you think I am conceited, then you are thoroughly mistaken. I have no inflated view of myself. Quite the contrary. I decide carefully what I want, and then I work towards it. This book reflects that ethos.

You truly can be a master trader. You truly can live in the house you desire, with the cars you desire in the drive. BUT you must believe me when I say that in order to get what you want, you need to think like the 1%. In fact, you don't even *need* to think like the 1%. You just need to *not* think like the 99%.

The following trade is a good example of how mindset trumps technical analysis any day of the week. In this example I short the German DAX 30 Index.

I get stopped out for a loss. I kick myself, because my stop-loss gets exceeded by a point or so, only to reverse back in my favour. My stop was too tight. Rather than lose my composure, I dismiss it.

Let me pause for a second. Do you know why some athletes let out a shout of frustration when they are not performing well? I thought about it for a while, after I saw Serena Williams shout when she lost an important point in a Wimbledon tennis final.

I think they let out a cry because it is a way to *reset* the mind, to come back into balance and get into the zone again. The act of letting out a cry helps them get rid of the frustration and find their inner peace and balance again.

I re-enter a short position at 14,479.80. The screenshot below is from the time of the trade.

		Amount	Open Price	Current Price	Open P/L
Germany 30	Sell	200	12479.8	12478.5	€ 260.00
Wall Street 30	Sell	200	27044	27046	–$500.00

The chart at the time of the trade looks as shown in Figure 1.

The DAX had gapped up. Did you know that only 48% of all gaps get filled on the same trading day?

By the third trading day after the gap, 76% of gaps were filled. Why am I telling you this? Don't believe trading books stating that all gaps get filled. They do not!

I short the DAX because the second bar on the chart is an inside bar – from the first ten-minute bar at the open. The third bar closes below the lowest point of the inside bar. Now I have a sell signal, because the first bar's high is at the same price as a prior high – a double top. I have a stop-loss in place. I have done my job as a trader. I have identified a low-risk entry point, and I have placed my stop-loss.

At this point in time, I am at the mercy of the markets. Maybe this will be a great trade. Maybe it won't. Who knows? No one knows. Before I carry on, I would like to ask YOU a question. It is a question for you to ponder upon.

Say you believe in the whole risk-to-reward argument, and you decide that you have a 40-point profit target. You decide upon a 40-point profit target because you risked 20 points. So, you argue that risk-to-reward is 2:1, two units of profit for one unit of risk, which sounds good.

It all sounds great, and there is virtually no textbook on trading that would argue against it. But I am arguing against it. I want to ask you some simple questions.

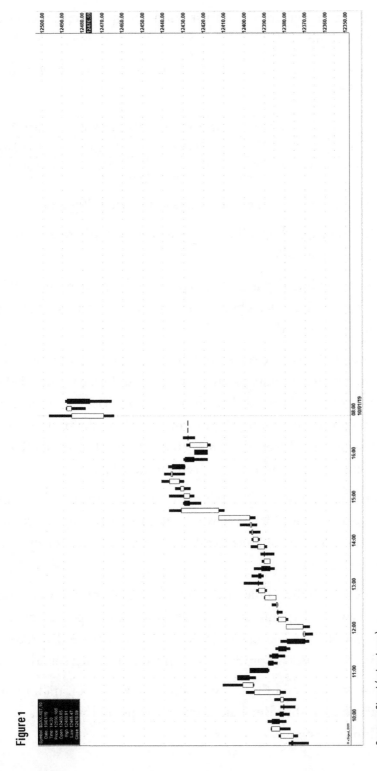

Figure 1

Source: eSignal (esignal.com)

If you make 40 points on this short position, and the market continues in your favour, how will you feel? How will you feel if a few hours later you see the market down a further 100 points from your exit?

I think the risk-to-reward concept has been designed by an academic who does not understand risk and the mind's association with risk. I think this academic has created a method to keep his mind at peace, in order to avoid pain.

Fifty minutes later the DAX is filling the gap. This is shown in Figure 2. The position is in profit.

A colleague of mine has followed my trade. The chart is looking good for us. We are in a conversation about the trade. It goes like this:

> **Friend:** I am tempted to take my profit. Do you have a target for this trade?
>
> **Tom:** Amigo, I don't trade with targets. Let's see what the market will give us. Stop-loss is at breakeven. We can't lose.
>
> **Friend:** Yes, I know. But yesterday was a poor day of trading. I lost 150 points. I read the market poorly. I had an idea, and the idea didn't work out. Either way, I lost 150 points. If I close my DAX position right now, I can make up for the lost trade this morning, and I can recover a lot of the points lost yesterday.
>
> What do you think?
>
> **Tom:** I think you are trading yesterday's experience. You haven't wiped the mind-slate clean. You are not present. You are focused on the past. You are trying to get back to an emotional equilibrium. You are in a state of imbalance because you are unable to shake the loss from yesterday. As a result, you are not judging the trade on its own merit, but on the merit of a past trade. You are not seeing the world as it is. You are seeing it as you are.
>
> I understand it is a soothing thought to close the trade. However, we are not trading to break even. We are trading to make money.

Figure 2

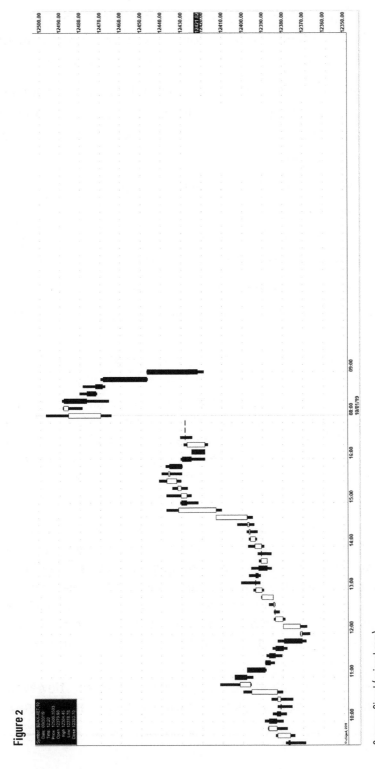

Source: eSignal (esignal.com)

Can you appreciate that trading is a mind game? It is a game of nerves. My friend was understandably shaken from his loss yesterday. He carried the loss over to the next day. It affected his decision making.

Back in 2007 I was invited to the Wimbledon tennis final. My friend was a big name in the media industry, and none other than Ralph Lauren had invited her to the tennis final – with a guest. So, there I was in the VIP tent, and I got to sit next to Luke Donald, who at the time was one of the best golfers in the world.

He is a softly spoken man, and very polite. We got talking about Tiger Woods, and I asked him a pretty to-the-point question about competing with Tiger.

"Is Tiger Woods a better golfer than you?"

I found his answer so incredibly insightful that I never forgot it. He said:

> I don't think Tiger is a better golfer than me, if you measure it in how well we putt, or how far we hit the ball, but Tiger Woods does have an amazing ability to forget his mistakes and move on.

> For example, we can be on the 15th and both make a bad putt. By the time we get to tee up on the 16th, it is as if Tiger has wiped his mind of whatever happened on the 15th, and he is totally in the moment.

> I, on the other hand, will still deal with the mistake I made on the 15th, and it will affect my performance on the 16th.

That is a truly insightful perspective of what really separates the very best in a chosen field. It is the *mind*, and what it processes at any given moment in time. Is it working *with* you or *against* you?

COGNITIVE DISSONANCE

My friend is having a ping-pong dialogue in his head, arguing for and against taking profits. I am no stranger to that conversation. I may have many years of trading experience, but I still have those thoughts in my head. I am just mindful of them when they arrive. When they do, I focus on the chart and what it is telling me. I don't look at the profit and loss (P&L).

What my friend is experiencing is known as cognitive dissonance. In the field of psychology, cognitive dissonance is the mental discomfort – psychological stress – experienced by an individual who simultaneously holds two contradictory beliefs or ideas in their head.

This discomfort is triggered by a situation in which a person's belief clashes with new evidence contradicting that belief. When confronted with facts that contradict beliefs, ideals, and values, people will try to find a way to resolve the contradiction to reduce their discomfort.

The best way for your rational mind to resolve the discomfort of a profitable position is to close it. The best way for the rational mind to resolve the discomfort of a losing position is to let it run.

In his 1957 book, *A Theory of Cognitive Dissonance*, author Leon Festinger proposed that human beings strive for internal psychological consistency to function mentally in the real world. He says that a person who experiences internal inconsistency tends to become psychologically uncomfortable and is motivated to reduce the cognitive dissonance.

One way to achieve the goal of reducing the discomfort is by making changes to justify the stressful behaviour, either by adding new unsubstantiated or irrelevant information to the cognition, or by avoiding circumstances and contradictory information likely to increase the magnitude of the cognitive dissonance.

In my friend's case, he is conflicted. He is associating pain with the performance of yesterday. He has an opportunity to eradicate the pain by closing his profitable position right now. The way he justifies this reasoning is by ignoring the information the market is giving him about his position. The market participants agree that the market should be sold short, but instead of acknowledging this, he is ignoring it.

From a logical point of view, this all makes sense. From an emotional point of view, this is an inconsistent approach to trading. Our trades from yesterday have no bearing on the markets today.

It is a new day. It is a new set of circumstances. Yet to most people's minds, the two trading days are connected. To our minds we are continuing today what we did yesterday. "Why wouldn't we be?" we tell ourselves.

Are you telling me that you can 'reset' your emotions every morning? Are you telling me that you can go to bed at night after a blazing row with your loved ones, and wake up reset and emotionally in equilibrium?

I doubt it; at least, not without a conscious effort. It is for this reason that I warm up ahead of the trading day by going through a process. We cover that later in the book. It is, after all, what the book is about. It is a *recipe book* for methods to avoid the pitfalls that the 90% experience.

Now, what is the source of my friend's turmoil? It is fear. Pure and simple. He is afraid he will lose what he has made on paper. He is desperate to get back to an emotional state where he is at peace. He is no longer trading the charts. He is no longer trading the markets. He is trading his own mental wellbeing.

FEAR

My friend is fearful. He is afraid that the money he lost yesterday will not be offset by the good trade he has going now. He is afraid that the profits he is currently experiencing will diminish, or in the worst case disappear.

He acknowledges that he can't lose on the trade. The stop-loss is now at breakeven. Unfortunately, that gives him little comfort.

I once saw a quote that made me smile: everything you ever wanted lives on the other side of fear. Yet fear is a necessity in our lives. The human brain is a product of millions of years of evolution, and we are hardwired with instincts that helped our ancestors to survive. We need fear to ensure survival in certain situations, but many of the fears that we carry are not appropriate for our trading.

Our minds have a primary function, which is to protect us against pain. If you introduce big drastic changes in your life, you are likely going to come face to face with that pain. A clever way to build staying power during change is to introduce that change slowly.

Say you set yourself the ambitious target of running a marathon. You achieve this goal by building up your body and mind for the task. Trading big size is exactly the same process. You need to give your mind time to learn to handle the mental anguish that comes from losing when the stakes are bigger.

There is no point in comparing yourself with others. Sure, take inspiration from others; but know this is a personal journey, and your job is to achieve an equilibrium mindset, no matter what size you are trading.

PHILIPPE PETIT

I saw a documentary about Philippe Petit a long time ago. Petit was a French artist who strapped a wire between the two World Trade Center buildings and then walked across it – several times.

What struck me about the incredible feat was the preparation.

It took Philippe some seven years of physical and mental training to accomplish the feat. Did you think he just set off and hoped for the best? No. In fact his original training height was quite modest compared to the altitudes he would eventually reach.

Philippe Petit is a fascinating character; he is someone who has had to deal with fear at a level beyond that which the rest of us have. I have learned a lot about fear and identifying my own shortcomings by studying his approach to his craft.

VISUALISATION

"Before my high-wire walk across the Seine to the second story of the Eiffel Tower, the seven-hundred-yard-long inclined cable looked so steep, the shadow of fear so real, I worried. Had there been an error in rigging calculations?"

How does Petit overcome these doubts?

With a simple visualisation exercise.

"On the spot I vanquished my anxiety by imagining the best outcome: my victorious last step above a cheering crowd of 250,000."

Added to this, Petit exaggerates his fears. Rather than try to muscle through or outwit fear, he suggests taming it by building it up so that when you are finally faced with your fear, you will be disappointed by how mundane the threat really is:

A clever tool in the arsenal to destroy fear: if a nightmare taps you on the shoulder, do not turn around immediately expecting to be scared. Pause and expect more, exaggerate.

Be ready to be very afraid, to scream in terror. The more delirious your expectation, the safer you will be when you see that reality is much less horrifying than what you had envisioned. Now turn around. See? It was not that bad – and you're already smiling.

He goes on to say that he has fears like everyone else. In particular, he talks about his dislike of spiders:

On the ground I profess to know no fear, but I lie. I will confess, with self-mockery, to arachnophobia and cynophobia [fear of dogs]. Because I see fear as an absence of knowledge, it would be simple for me to conquer such silly terrors.

"I am too busy these days," I'll say, "but when I decide it's time to get rid of my aversion to animals with too many legs (or not enough legs—snakes are not my friends, either), I know exactly how to proceed."

I will read science reports, watch documentaries, visit the zoo. I will interview spider-wranglers (is there such a profession?) to discover how these creatures evolved, how they hunt, mate, sleep, and, most importantly, what frightens the hairy, scary beast. Then, like James Bond, I won't have any problem having a tarantula dance on my forearm.

Petit's walk remains one of the most fabled – and stunning – acts of public art ever. He says there was no *why* behind the act. To quote his own words:

To me, it is really simple. Life should be lived on the edge of life. You have to exercise rebellion, to refuse to tape yourself to rules, to refuse your own success, to refuse to repeat yourself, to see every day, every year, every idea as a true challenge, and then you are going to live your life on a tightrope.

THE EGO, AND WONDERFUL FAILURE

I am not a fan of clichés. They display a lack of original thought. I am quite cynical towards those who peddle clichés. It doesn't sit well with me to hear people say that I should run my profits and cut my losses. Yes, but how do I deal with the fear of running my profits?

It doesn't sit well with me when a female friend tells me she is in an abusive relationship, and another friend chirps in and dismissively states that the solution is to "just leave the bastard." It is a platitude. It is factually true, but it is nonsense, nevertheless.

When a solution is obvious, the problem is rarely the only problem. You might as well tell an alcoholic to just stop drinking. There is a reason he is drinking, and there is a reason he is struggling to stop.

Does *failure* exist? I come from a home where you rarely received praise for your achievements. They were expected. The failures, on the other hand, were pointed out – and not in a constructive manner.

I had to retrain my mind to stop being afraid of making mistakes. I used to have a favourite saying as a child: "It is not my fault". Today the buck stops with me every time. It is always my fault. I am good at making mistakes, so that I can learn from them.

Failure is a friend in life – if you tell your mind that it is okay to fail. I participate in a radio programme about trading and investments. The focal point of the show is the competition between two other traders and me.

The competition is always fierce, and every week we are questioned about the content of our portfolios. My trading style is quite black and white. If I think the market is headed lower, I will buy some put options or some bear certificates, and vice-versa if I am bullish.

I learned a long time ago that the best way to shut down a journalist is to be 100% honest. So, when the radio host baits me by saying "Uhm Tom, you got that one wrong, huh?", the worst thing I can do is to start defending myself. If I start making excuses or argue a defensive stance, I simply pour petrol on that fire.

It is such a great metaphor for life. Own up to your errors and be done with it. So, when the radio host is trying to engage in a line of questioning aimed at getting me to defend myself, I always double down in the opposite direction by saying something like, "Oh my lord, I don't think I could have been more wrong, even if I tried," or "Oh boy, even a five-year-old could have done better than me."

TRADING MIND UPSIDE-DOWN

From my research into the behaviour of our clients during my years at City Index, I concluded that the overwhelming majority had an unhealthy mental thought pattern. They would feel fear at times where there was no reason to be fearful. This would manifest during times in which their positions were making money.

However I manipulate the argument, it is still a fear of losing. In this case it is the fear of losing the profits accrued on paper.

When the clients were in losing positions, they would be reluctant to realise the loss. It was as if they had the attitude that as long as the position was open, it might still come good. As I see it, they opted to replace fear with hope. They hoped the losing position would come back to breakeven.

Going back to the DAX example, my friend hung on to the trade. I did my best to guide him through the pain. He moved his stop-loss down. It meant he had some profits to show for it, if the market moved back up again.

In my experience if you can guide a person through a successful trade, where he or she holds on to the trade, you will begin to create the right kind of neuro-associations. The trader will experience the thrill of holding on to a trade. They will experience the joy of locking in more and more profits.

My friend was over the moon with the development of the chart. However, it was quite clear that he was constantly looking for reasons to take profit. The thought of leaving money on the table did not sit well with him at all.

To his credit he held on to the trade, spurred on by my conviction that the market showed nothing but weakness. We were soon rewarded by a sudden liquidity vacuum. I try not to get excited when the market is giving me a windfall. However, at times even I will have to fist pump the air, even though I am alone in my office.

The whole trade sequence is displayed in the time-stamped records in my Telegram channel under 1 October 2019. See Figure 3.

ELON MUSK

I am not a fan of Tesla. This is due to the fact I shorted it and lost big. Yes, I know. What a silly argument, considering Teslas are seemingly good cars.

I am a fan of Elon Musk, however. We are bound to make mistakes in life, but mistakes are like fuel for the rocket of improvement. Talking of rockets, how do you think people like Elon Musk handle failure?

He is trying to accomplish incredible, life-changing things – things like the electrification of automobiles and the colonisation of space – and he does it while the whole world is watching.

Figure 3

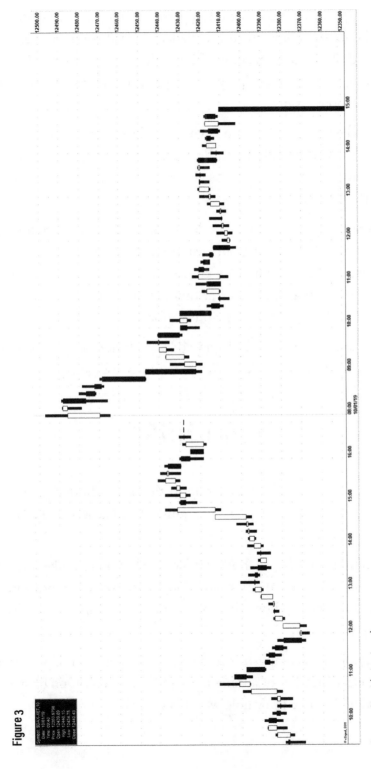

Source: eSignal (esignal.com)

For him the possibility of failure is ever present. Not only that, but when he fails it becomes spectacular headline news. Yet Musk just keeps on going and going, doing things that are extremely risky but also extremely important.

How does he handle his fear of failure? Does he even fear failure at all, or is he somehow hardwired with resilience against this form of anxiety?

Apparently not. Musk has publicly stated he feels fear quite strongly. So how does he keep going despite this terror?

There are two main elements to Musk's ability to overcome his fears. The first is an overwhelming passion for his projects. He admits that SpaceX was an insane venture, but he had a compelling reason for pushing ahead:

> I had concluded that if something didn't happen to improve rocket technology, we'd be stuck on earth forever. People sometimes think technology just automatically gets better every year but actually it doesn't. It only gets better if smart people work like crazy to make it better.
>
> By itself, technology, if people don't work at it, actually will decline. Look at, say, ancient Egypt, where they were able to build these incredible pyramids and then they basically forgot how to build pyramids... There are many such examples in history... entropy is not on your side.

Elon Musk was not prepared to sit idly by and watch history repeat itself.

The second element is what Musk calls *fatalism*. Just focusing on why you're taking a scary risk isn't always enough to overcome hesitation. It wasn't for Musk:

> Something that can be helpful is fatalism, to some degree. If you just accept the probabilities, then that diminishes fear. When starting SpaceX, I thought the odds of success were less than ten

percent and I just accepted that actually probably I would just lose everything. But that maybe we would make some progress.

He is not the only one to use this approach. Visualising the worst-case scenario can make us appreciate objectively what we are trying to achieve. Facing our fears removes their power over us.

Have I digressed too far from the trading journey ahead?

I don't think so. I draw inspiration from many sources, both in and outside of the trading world: Kobe Bryant, Rafa Nadal, Cristiano Ronaldo, Sergio Ramos and Charlie Munger, to name a few.

Very different people, yet all obsessed with the journey, the enrichment of their lives and the perfection of their craft. Studying their approach to their work suggests they found the thing they would love to do even if they didn't get paid for it. I am sure they are businessmen too, and I am sure they keep an eye on the dollars coming in. However, it feels like they perform their craft for the love of it.

DO YOU WANT IT BAD?

How bad do you want it? Is this journey for you? I don't know. Only you can answer that. Permit me to ask you a question: what is the alternative?

You are reading these pages because you want to trade well. Perhaps you have been in my live trading room, and you have seen what my trading philosophy is doing for me. You want to learn more. I applaud that.

Perhaps it is time to acknowledge trading for what it is? It is a great way to expose all your flaws. It is a great way to highlight your strengths. Through my trading and my research, I have uncovered weaknesses in my character.

For me, the side benefit of earning a living from trading the financial markets is the character traits it instils in me. I am more patient than ever. I am much more focused and disciplined than I was before.

Failure is one of our greatest learning tools.

TIMES OF DOUBT

Do you really want to trade profitably? I have had to answer that a few times in my career. I have had to make some sacrifices along the way. I have been called out once by a coach who felt my effort was insincere.

I recently found myself having dinner with a friend. I have known him for 15 years. I met him when I gave a speech somewhere in the North of England. My friend had asked if he could consult with me while I was in Manchester to give a talk about trading, and naturally I agreed.

As we ate, he became very animated. At one point he knocked over a glass of water while expressing his frustration with his trading. It was difficult to really pinpoint what the problem was in his trading, because he never made any specific reference to a problem.

It was clear to me that he really was in distress and wanted help, but I was unable to figure out in what capacity my help should come. So, I offered him help in the one area that I felt was appropriate. I offered to go over his trading statements. As I see it, that is the only way I can really help someone. It is a lot of work, but at least I am getting a sense of who he is as a trader.

As we said our goodbyes, he told me he would send over his statements. I confirmed, and said I would look forward to hearing from him. As I write this, he has not emailed me. He has not written to me on message apps. Silence. Not a word.

If I am offered help in an area where I desperately want to excel, and the help comes from a friend who is an expert in the area, I will respond as soon as I can, if not immediately. As of some four to five days later, I haven't heard a peep.

How badly do you think he wants this? How desperate do you think he is? I question how much he really wants this. I have observed this pattern on several occasions. The student claims to be really keen, but in reality it is mere words.

It reminds me of a conversation that the famous trader Ed Seykota had with another brilliant trader and friend. The friend told Ed that he intended to coach a losing trader into a winning trader by teaching him some important pointers that were missing from his trading.

Ed Seykota paused for a second, and then said that the friend would fail to teach the student anything. He said that a losing trader is not going to wish to transform himself. That is the sort of thing that only winning traders do.

We can all ask for guidance from someone who is better than us. As the saying goes, you only get better by playing a better opponent. I have guided many that were already well on their way to trading with confidence. I merely refined and suggested.

Whether I will hear from my friend or not remains unknown. What is known is that many people open trading accounts in the hope of making money. Their effort is disproportional to their expectations, and their results are aligned with their effort. They simply don't work hard enough.

Before I move on to the next topic, I want to warn you: I am a trader who uses charts, but that doesn't mean that I believe charts are responsible for my profitable trading. I once read that technical analysts are afraid of heights. That is another way of saying that they are unable to let their winners run, because they keep seeing overhead resistance.

I have called the next chapter 'The Curse of Patterns', because I believe fully that as much as patterns help us, they also make our trading lives difficult. In the search for patterns, we see things that are simply not there.

THE CURSE OF PATTERNS

I F YOU STRIP away the time and price axis of a chart, you will likely be unable to differentiate between a five-minute chart and an hourly chart.

In a sense, that is good news. It means we can perfect our craft and then find a time frame that suits our trading temper. The trader with the ability to focus for long stretches of time will find the one-minute chart and the five-minute chart provide ample opportunity to make money.

The trader with time constraints will probably favour a longer time frame such as the hourly chart or the four-hour chart. It means he or she doesn't have to check the chart so frequently.

Charts are far superior to fundamental analysis when it comes to entry points and exit points, and I can use the same tools, irrespective of what time frame I am trading on.

Am I opposed to fundamental macroanalysis? I would be a fool if I dismissed the fundamentals. The two should not be in opposing camps. They should walk hand in hand, as they complement each other and make up for each other's flaws.

Now, I would not go so far as to say that chart analysis is the Holy Grail. Yes, I have made a lot of money from trading charts, but it was not my ability to read a chart that made me a wealthy trader.

I don't believe that there is a Holy Grail when it comes to trading, and I certainly don't believe that chart analysis is the Holy Grail.

PATTERNICITY

Apophenia is a Latin word that, translated into English, means *patternicity.* This is a behaviour centred around seeing things that aren't there; the tendency to perceive meaningful patterns and connections amongst unrelated events. Patternicity is often a harmless diversion. However, it can be used to support a belief that is otherwise lacking in evidence, like a conspiracy theory.

Our minds tend to seek out the information that confirms the bias that we have already decided upon. Therefore, to be completely objective in chart analysis is virtually impossible.

My early mentor Bryce Gilmore once commented on this fact. He said to me, "Tom, you only see in the markets and on charts what you have trained your eyes to see."

Another perspective of such wisdom was expressed by Anaïs Nin. She said, "We don't see things as they are, we see them as we are."

"What is the relevance to trading?" I hear you say. I had a friend a long time ago who had made a lot of money trading. Nick was a great trader, right up until 2004.

He started reading and believing some writers and contributors on Zero Hedge and he turned bearish on the stock market. He kept shorting. But the market kept going up. He just could not accept that there was no more downside after the bear market of 2000–2003. He didn't see the market as it was. He saw it as he was. He was negative. He had read that the bear market would continue. He stopped trading what he saw, and he let his opinion cloud his objectivity.

Nick no longer trades.

I didn't want to write a book on charts. There are so many books on technical analysis, written by people who I doubt trade full time. I think they tell themselves that because they have a trading account and because they trade from time to time, they are qualified to write books on trading.

Although I trade full time, I really don't think I could add anything new to the world of charting. Charting didn't make me money. Indicators never made me money. Ratios and bands never filled my bank account.

As I am about to post some charts, I want to point out to you that it is to prove a point, rather than to educate you on the merits of technical analysis.

THE TREND LINE FANATICAL

In the early stages of our chart journey, we come across trend lines. Trend lines are easy to use, and they give the appearance of a great trading strategy, especially when we do it *after the fact*.

Figure 4 shows a naked chart. The diligent chartist begins to draw trend lines. He or she has the full overview of the day.

Remember, the brain will have as its prime objective – I repeat, **PRIME OBJECTIVE** – to avoid you experiencing pain. A losing trade equals pain.

So, the brain sends a signal to the eyes to ignore the setups that do not work. This selection bias creates a distorted image of the validity of trend lines.

You can replace trend lines with any other analytical tool from your charting package, and the bias will remain in place: Fibonacci, Bollinger Bands, Keltner Channels, etc.

Figure 4

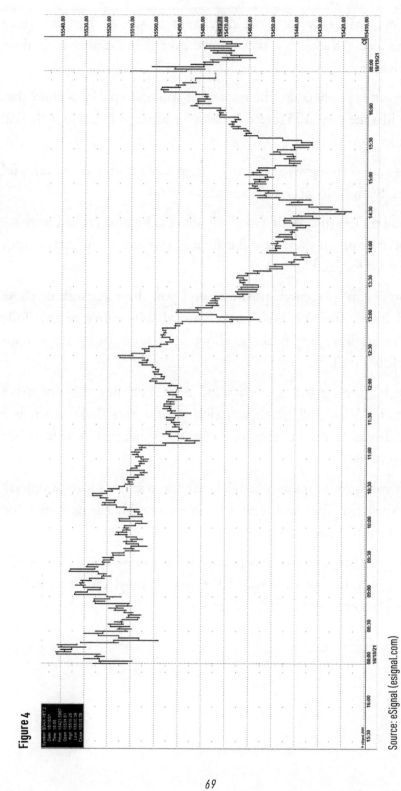

Source: eSignal (esignal.com)

Your eyes will only see what they want to see. At best they may *see* the losing trades, but they glance over them, diminishing their significance.

The result is predictable. The researcher will end up with a chart that looks like the one in Figure 5. It has a lot of trend line setups that all result in great trades.

There are no losing trades. Every single trade results in meaningful profits. Such is the power of our subconscious.

Cynical traders (people like me) will notice things other traders miss – not because others don't have the ability to see them, but because they don't want to. See Figure 6.

If you are in a research position, and you draw enough of these trend lines after the fact, you're most likely going to conclude that trend lines are nothing short of a fantastic tool, perhaps the Holy Grail.

There is nothing wrong with trend lines, but they will not make you rich. What will make you rich is how you think when you trade. If you think like everyone else, then your results will be like everyone else's.

Don't you want to make money? Don't you want to separate yourself from the herd? Then realise that trading profitably has nothing to do with the instrument you use.

In order to prove to you how pointless it is to research tools, I would like to introduce you to two of the world's most esteemed traders, Larry Pesavento and Larry Williams.

Figure 5

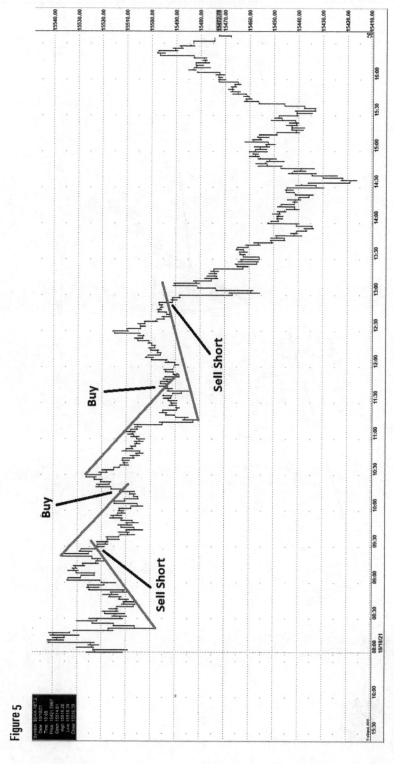

Source: eSignal (esignal.com)

Figure 6

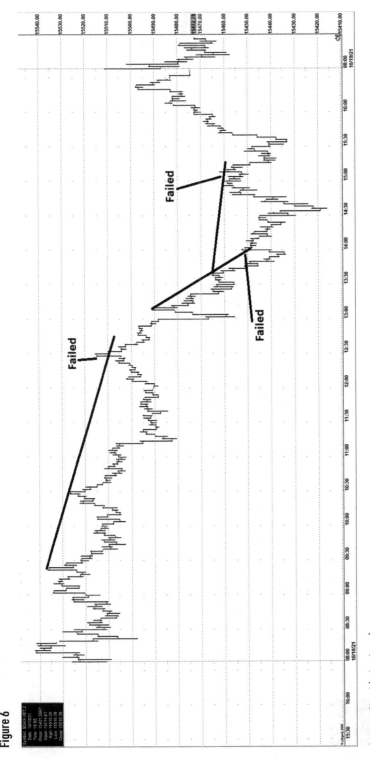

Source: eSignal (esignal.com)

LARRY PESAVENTO VERSUS LARRY WILLIAMS

The two Larrys are both in their senior years. They are both Americans, and incidentally they are friends. Both of them have enjoyed trading careers spanning decades. Both of them have made their living from trading.

Larry Pesavento is famous for his use of patterns and Fibonacci ratios. Larry Williams is famous for his pattern recognition setups. Both have written several books on their chosen tools.

In a workshop I organised back in 2005, Larry Williams – who was one of the speakers – showed statistics from the S&P 500 Index, which depicted all the major retracements on an hourly chart spanning a decade.

As you can imagine, there was virtually every single conceivable percentage retracement on display. What did not stand out, though, was 61.8% or 38.2% – the two prominent Fibonacci ratios. Sure, they were there, but they were surrounded by masses of other percentages.

Yes, it turns out the magical growth sequence of Fibonacci does not, after all, rule the market. So how come it works for Larry Pesavento? The answer is simple: it doesn't have to work all the time to make it a profitable strategy.

In Oslo, Norway, in 2016 I gave a talk on Fibonacci ratios. For the talk I had researched all occurrences in which the German DAX Index retraced 78.6% – the square root of 0.618 – and I proved that although the 78.6% retracement had a hit rate of 20%, it could still be a useful strategy. You had to risk very little and go for big pay-outs for it to work.

S&P 500 & FIBONACCI

The S&P 500 enjoyed an 11% rally during the summer months of 2021. The index rallied from 4,050 to 4,550. Along the way, as you can see on the next chart, there were three significant retracements. The role of the Fibonacci sequence is to enable us to buy into retracements at favourable retracement ratios, such as 38.2% retracement, 61.8% retracement, or even 78.6% retracement. See Figure 7.

What I am going to show you now is a simple demonstration of the power of hype and selection bias. See Figure 8.

Fibonacci ratios are one of the best-known tools in the trading arena. There is not a single one of these three major retracements in the S&P 500 Index that is identified by either 38.2%, 61,8% or even 78.6% ratios.

In fact, two ratios seem to come up more frequently: 43% retracement and 74% retracement. I put that down to randomness. Yes, such is the power of our belief system.

We want to believe there is a magical growth sequence to the way the financial markets expand and contract. We want to believe that there is a universal order to the markets, dictated by a higher deity who created the universe using the mathematical sequence of what we know as Fibonacci.

And it works just often enough to keep the believers believing. This is the danger of charts. When we research, we are looking for something to get us in on the long side, so we never miss a rally; or we look for something to make us sell short, so we never miss a short sell. We enter with a bias.

This is apophenia in play. Beware!

Figure 7

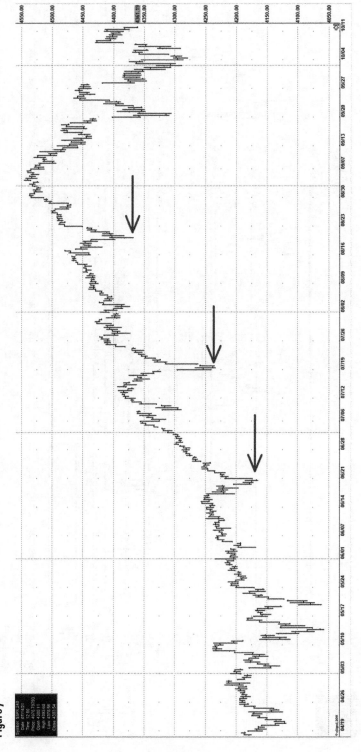

Source: eSignal (esignal.com)

Figure 8

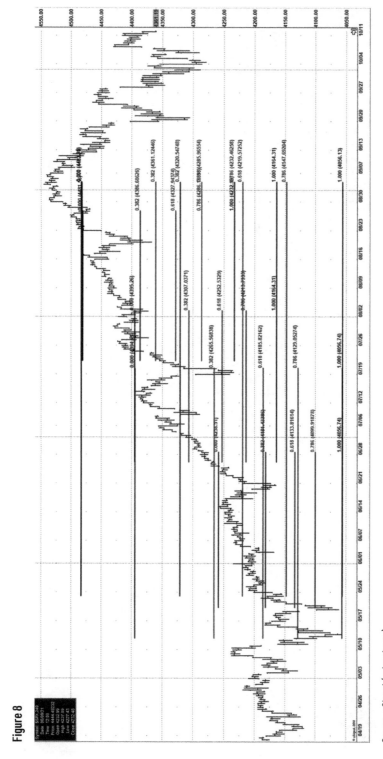

Source: eSignal (esignal.com)

DIVORCE RATES IN SPAIN

The definition of *ignorance* is a lack of knowledge or information. You can be a smart individual but be ignorant in some areas. For example, I am rather ignorant when it comes to, say, soulmates and flat Earth theory. You could argue that I am ignorant because I am not interested, or I don't believe in it.

Fair point. Specifically, on the point of finding your soulmate – the one-and-only whom you will spend eternity with, the person who is perfect for you in every shape or form – well, I don't believe they are real.

You see, as ignorant as I am in the ways of love, I can read statistics, and on that basis, I am supposed to conclude that soulmates have better chances of finding each other in certain countries? I don't think so!

For example, there are certainly not many self-confessed soulmates in Spain or Luxembourg. Did you know that there is a 65% divorce rate in Spain and an 87% divorce rate in Luxembourg?

There's only a 42% divorce rate in the UK. Does that mean that you have a higher chance of finding your soulmate if you live on the British Isles than in Spain?

Plenty of people believe that the sun's heavenly position relative to randomly defined stellar constellations at the time of my birth somehow affects my personality.

There are also people who believe that the markets are an equation to be solved, a code to be cracked. All of those people are delusional, or to put it more politely, they are ignorant.

THE FRAUD OF THE CANDLESTICK GURU

In order to avoid a lawsuit, I have blanked out the name of the central character in the following story. When candlestick charts became a hot topic in the 1990s, one person – who had been instrumental in the propagation of their use – was sitting in a restaurant somewhere in the world with another high-profile trader and me.

The central character had at the time published books on the use of candlestick charts. As we sat in the restaurant, I asked him if he believed that some of these patterns had to be identified by different names, when they were practically identical.

For example, I argued, the Harami pattern and the Harami Cross pattern are to all intents and purposes identical, except the Harami Cross pattern has no body, while the Harami pattern has one. However, they are both inside bar patterns.

It seemed to me like a deliberate attempt to inflate the number of patterns, for purely commercial reasons rather than for legitimate trading reasons. Many of the patterns are near identical but have different names.

I asked him if he had a favourite pattern he used, or a selection of preferred patterns he stuck to, and if so, what time frame he traded them on.

He answered that he wasn't trading the patterns. Not only that, but he also conceded that he didn't trade at all.

I don't know how you feel about that, but it doesn't sit very well with me. I immediately cut all ties with the gentleman. I felt as if his only mission was to invent as many patterns as he possibly could, in order to fill pages in books and courses, and create alerts on his trading software.

Am I arguing that candlestick charts are worthless? No. I just don't believe that there is statistical relevance to all the patterns.

I am not alone. A handful of academic research articles suggest the same. Here is the conclusion from one such article, 'A Statistical Analysis of the Predictive Power of Japanese Candlesticks', written by Mohamed Jamaloodeen, Adrian Heinz and Lissa Pollacia, and published in the *Journal of International & Interdisciplinary Business Research* in June 2018:

> Japanese Candlesticks is a technique for plotting past price action of a specific underlying such as a stock, index or commodity using open, high, low and close prices. These candlesticks create patterns believed to forecast future price movement. Although the candles' popularity has increased rapidly over the last decade, there is still little statistical evidence about their effectiveness over a large number of occurrences. In this work, we analyze the predictive power of the Shooting Star and Hammer patterns using over six decades of historical data of the S&P 500 Index. In our studies, we found out that historically these patterns have offered little forecasting reliability when using closing prices.

In another work by Piyapas Tharavanij, Vasan Siraprapasiri and Kittichai Rajchamaha, the researchers conclude the following:

> This article investigates the profitability of candlestick patterns. The holding periods are one, three, five, and ten days. This study tests the predictive power of bullish and bearish candlestick reversal patterns both without technical filtering and with technical filtering (stochastics [%D], Relative Strength Index [RSI], Money Flow Index [MFI]) by applying the skewness adjusted t test and the binomial test.

> The statistical analysis finds little use of both bullish and bearish candlestick reversal patterns since the mean returns of most patterns are not statistically different from zero.

Even the ones with statistically significant returns do have high risks in terms of standard deviations. The binomial test results also indicate that candlestick patterns **cannot** reliably predict market directions. In addition, this article finds that filtering by %D, RSI, or MFI generally does not increase profitability nor prediction accuracy of candlestick patterns.

TRADERS BEWARE

Brokers and educators have put the cart before the horse. They make us think that learning as many patterns as we possibly can will increase our chances of trading success. This is simply not true. The more patterns we know, the more we are inclined to talk ourselves out of good positions.

There is nothing wrong with technical analysis and patterns, and candle formation and indicators and ratios and bands. Yes, I don't believe in many of them, because they are subjective and don't hold up under real scrutiny. But then again, trading is so subjective anyway that we don't need to be right very much to make a good living from trading.

AN OLD FOX TELLS

My friend Trevor Neil ran a hedge fund that had a 25% hit rate on their trades. I want to tell you his story here to give you some deeper insight into how some of the best professional traders work and think. I hope you will find it illuminating.

It should also serve as a reminder that there are many ways to make money in the market. Your job is not to follow someone, but to find a way that you like, that resonates with you and who you are and what you like to do.

The story starts with me asking Trevor a question. I knew that he had been associated with Tom DeMark and his Sequential indicator. Tom DeMark is something of a legend within the technical analysis world.

I happen to have met DeMark myself at a Bloomberg lunch many years ago. He seemed like a nice guy, although I had very little to ask him, as I was unfamiliar with his work. You see, his work was only available to those who had a Bloomberg terminal.

The Bloomberg terminal at that time was some $25,000 a year. Today, though, Tom DeMark's work is available on many trading platforms, in case you are interested.

I asked Trevor about the Sequential indicator, and his eyes lit up. He told me a story about how he and his friend had decided that there was an edge to be gained from trading the Sequential indicator on a very short-term time frame.

They moved to South Africa and started trading South African shares on a *one-minute chart*. I have never heard of a professional outfit, with significant funds under management, trade on such a short time frame.

However, that is not what impressed me most about the story. What impressed me most was how they managed to make money on what other traders would consider an abysmal hit rate.

Most people believe that you have to deploy a trading strategy that has a hit rate better than 50%. Trevor told me that their results varied. There were times when they were hot, and there were times when they were not.

When they were hot, the hit rate would push 40%. When they were not, the hit rate was down in the mid-20s.

Overall, though, they had in their hands a tool that generated about 25–30 winning trades out of every 100 trades placed. They were wildly successful.

They traded the fund for a handful of years, then they returned the capital to the investors. They had made their money, and as neither of them were spring chickens, they decided enough was enough. It was time to go home and spend quality time with their families. Had they been younger, they probably would have continued.

Now I don't know about you, but I like the story. It reaffirms the idea that I have about trading. How you think when you trade is much more important than whether your strategy has a hit rate in the 50s or in the 70s or in the 90s.

While the story is not conclusive evidence that anyone can make money trading, as long as they have the proper money management rules and the required patience, it is a brilliant anecdote of two traders being able to make money even though – from a conventional point of view – their strategy on paper should not have generated a profit.

So, what was the secret?

Well, the answer is simple. Although they lost 75 out of 100 trades, those 25 winning trades more than surpassed in profits what the 75 trades generated in losses. Trevor told me that they expected to make 25 times in profit what the risk was. He also told me that when they executed a trade, they expected it to work immediately. So, I grilled him a little bit on that point.

"What do you mean you expected it to work immediately?" I said. He said he meant exactly that: when they executed a trade, they expected the trade to begin to work immediately. If they had bought at 50, they would not want it to go to 48. If it went to 48, they would stop themselves out.

It meant they had plenty of small losses. Their back-testing had shown that if the strategy was to be traded correctly, it would work immediately. If it didn't work immediately, the strategy called for the position to be closed.

BELIEVE AND ACT

When you can act and perform without any fear of consequences and repercussions, you are trading from an ideal state. When you consider how many people lose money overall in trading, you logically have to conclude that achieving this state is not an easy undertaking. It would be foolish to think that this state of mind comes easily or even naturally. It doesn't.

I once sat and traded for a few months with a guy from Germany. He possessed an almost superhuman ability to do nothing. His patience was unrivalled. While we traded together I made it a sport to be as patient as he was.

It was fun and, dare I say, somewhat painful. I missed many a good trade, but the ones I took outweighed all the others.

You must be patient with yourself. You must be able to let your knowledge settle and mature within you. If you trade small size now, but you want to trade bigger size in the future, then that journey will most likely be anything but linear.

It will be a journey of progress and setbacks. It will be a journey of progress and status quo. I can guarantee you that. You have to grow into the trader you dream of becoming.

You must be patient with your trade entries. You must be patient with yourself. If you can bring those two qualities to the table, then the rest will solve itself in time. You will grow your trade size at a pace where your mind will not be alarmed or fearful.

I discuss this in much greater detail towards the end of the book. Otherwise, I am just like the well-meaning friend who says to my alcoholic friend, "Well, just stop drinking."

Sure, if only it were that easy. Likewise, me saying to you "Just have more patience" is about as helpful as a hog roast at a vegan convention.

One macro trader I deeply admire is Greg Coffey, an outstanding London hedge fund trader. In a piece in a newspaper one client described him as "humble and arrogant in equal measures – the perfect trader".

The piece went on to describe that Coffey had an absolute conviction on his trades, to the point of being arrogant, *but* he was equally quick to be humble when the trades didn't work out well.

Remember this saying:

It is not what you know that kills you. It is what you think you know, but which just isn't so, that kills you.

THE NATURE OF THE GAME

The game never changes, and it never will. Algorithms won't change the game. Laws won't change the game. Because this is an inner game, and you need to spend time – maybe not as much time as you do on charts, but a huge amount of time – contemplating what human qualities you are bringing to the game of trading.

Moving in the right direction comes from knowledge of yourself and an understanding of the markets. The game never changes. The players change, of course. We all grow old and die, and we are replaced with fresh blood. Sadly, people don't change, unless they make an out-of-the-ordinary effort to do so.

We have a reptile mind, which is not fond of change. "Hey, if it ain't broke, why do you want to fix it?" Well, because it *is* broken. I am not making money how I know I can, so I want to change that. If that means I have to learn to live under a different paradigm, and have a different perspective on fear and hope, so be it.

THE ROLE OF CHARTS

You can't create a master painting with just one colour. You don't create a Michelin-star meal with just one ingredient. And you most certainly do not create a viable business as a trader by only focusing on charts.

The role of the chart is to give you a visual representation of the thoughts of other market participants. It enables me to be much more specific in my entry and exit criteria than, say, a fundamental trader.

However, it is easy to get seduced by the randomness of charts. Over time, though, it is not your chart reading skills that will decide the number of zeros on your trading account.

Controlling your mind is no easy task. Your reflex mind will jump to conclusions before your conscious, reflective mind has had a moment to really consider your response.

The sole purpose of this book is to provide you with the right tools to program your mind to be a trader – a profitable one.

Our minds are feeble creatures, if left unchecked. Whenever I give a talk about the role of psychology in trading, I always show people the logo of Federal Express, and then I ask them: "Where is the arrow?"

In case you didn't know already, take a look at the FedEx logo – there is an arrow hidden between the 'E' and the 'x'.

The coordination between the eyes and the mind is fascinating. The eyes can see one thing, while the reactive impulse mind tells us that we are seeing something else.

It is only through observance and training that we become mindful of our tendency to believe what we immediately *think* we see.

Consider the following image. Which square on this chequerboard is darker, A or B?

You might be surprised to learn that both squares are exactly the same shade of grey, though it is very likely that your mind told you that square A is darker. Published by MIT professor Edward H. Adelson in 1995, this optical illusion perfectly demonstrates how the mind can misinterpret information passed to it by the eyes.

Another example you may have encountered before is a little harder to demonstrate in this book, but I will explain how it played out in the speech I gave – which gave me the impetus to write this book. It is a mind-flexibility exercise.

I showed the audience a simple image: a red square. I asked them to call out the colour of the image. "Red!" they shouted in unison.

Simple enough, right? I then removed the red square and revealed a yellow one. Same result: "Yellow!"

I swapped in a green square. "Green!" they cried.

Red. Yellow. Green. So far, so good.

The audience didn't even need to think about it; that is how dominant the automatic response system is.

Then we moved onto the trickier bit. I showed the audience an image of the word *red* written in blue ink, and asked what colour that image was.

A lot of them called out "Red!"

I showed them *yellow* written in red ink. Some called out "Red!" but I heard far more shouts of "Yellow!"

We repeated this process with a series of colour names written in ink of a different colour. Over time, the audience responses became more consistently accurate. Through a humorous exercise I established that our eyes and minds do not necessarily work in a coordinated manner. Our brain, seeing the word *red*, wants us to say "red" – even when the answer to the question is "blue". It is as if we consciously need to stop the brain from jumping to conclusions.

This is an important trait in trading, because we often see things that are literally not there.

Charts do not work as well in real time as *after the fact*. Unfortunately, you have to believe and act.

If you struggle with that after a few failed trades, then that is your brain trying to protect you against pain. You will begin to second guess your signals, and you will sabotage your own best interests. I have been there. I have done it. And I have the cure.

GOOD TRADING GOES AGAINST HUMAN NATURE

When I make speeches about trading, in person or on YouTube, I often talk about the concepts of *value* and *price*. What is something worth?

I think my old car is worth £10,000. The car dealer feels it is worth £8,000. Who do you think is going to win that argument, if I am keen to sell?

What something is worth is an emotional, biased statement. Price, on the other hand, is where buyers and sellers meet. It doesn't make much sense to say that something is worth more.

You can anticipate that something will be worth more or less in the future. I mean, that is the essence of the mechanics of my job. Psychology aside, I buy in the hope that whatever I buy will rise in price.

Heraclitus, the pre-Socratic Greek philosopher, said: "No man ever steps in the same river twice, for it's not the same river and he's not the same man." That is important to bear in mind as a speculator, because the market changes constantly.

Mankind has an ambivalent attitude to change. We want change, because otherwise our lives become mundane and boring; but if the change is thrust upon us, rather than driven by motivation and enthusiasm, then we tend to resent it.

The first time I became aware of the importance of mindset in trading was upon reading a book about the trading life of an anonymous trader called Phantom of the Pit. It is a free book. You can find it with my own notes on www.tradertom.com – in the resource section.

In the book the mystery trader argues that behaviour modification is the single most important concept in trading. The ability to change one's mind without causing a mental disequilibrium is the single most important ability for a trader.

Running a live Telegram trading channel means I am constantly asked questions – the majority of them from inexperienced traders. One persistent question I get asked is: "Why are you trading against the trend?"

When I get asked such a question, I smile, because it is both a naïve and innocent question. It is naïve because *any* trader can be accused of trading against the trend.

It simply depends on the time frame you are looking at. If you are a five-minute candle trader, you don't care that the trend on the weekly chart is down. You care about the trend of the five-minute chart.

Another reason why it is naïve is because the whole construct of technical analysis is fraught with contradictions.

Think about it.

You are asked to follow the trend; but what happens when you sell a double top? You are betting against the trend. The same can be argued for a double bottom. You are buying a market that is moving down.

THIRTY YEARS OF DATA

I am a day trader. My speciality is stock indices such as the Dow Jones Index. I looked at the statistics of closing prices in the index over the last 30 years. That equates to roughly 7,500 trading days. I wanted to know how often the Dow Index closed higher for the day and how often it closed lower for the day compared to the previous day's closing price.

I had an idea that, since the Dow Index over the last 30 years had risen from 3,300 to nearly 36,000, you could expect more positive closing prices than negative closing prices. I was wrong in that assumption.

Over the last 30 years only 50.4% of all closing prices were higher than the previous day's closing price. This means the distribution of *plus days* and *minus days* in the Dow Index is evenly distributed.

The ramifications of this statistic is that day traders like me can't rely too much on the *trend* on the higher time frame, because virtually anything can happen down on the five-minute chart.

The challenge traders face can be summed up very easily, in a Heraclitus-style explanation. When we shop for a pint of milk, we know that milk is a uniform product. It doesn't matter where on God's green earth you shop for a pint of milk. Milk is milk.

Hence, if milk costs twice as much in one supermarket as opposed to another supermarket, you can again rightly conclude that a pint of milk is expensive in one supermarket, and it is cheap in the other supermarket.

However, a share, or a currency, or a share index, is like a river. It is in constant transformation. The transformation is the result of the interaction of traders and investors.

Their action is the result of their opinions about the future. You may agree with their opinions, or you may disagree; but to say that the majority are wrong is counterproductive to efficient money-making in the markets.

There are many part-time traders who are incredibly successful in their other careers but struggle when it comes to trading. What we have to do to succeed in the world of trading is significantly different to what we have to do to succeed in the world outside of it.

For example, if you go into a supermarket to buy dinner, and you see that there is a special offer on chicken, you will be inclined to take advantage of this offer. If chicken is offered at half price, then you might be thinking that this is a great price, and you will want to buy some supply for the freezer.

Our human nature is such that we love a bargain. We love to seek out good offers and take advantage of them. It fills us with a sense of joy to know we have bought something which is cheap.

Just yesterday I went shopping and there was an aisle with discounted items. Everything was half price or less. I bought soap and washing liquid and detergent for the next 12 months.

As I filled the trolley, I laughed to myself, mostly because I knew that I would go on to write a chapter about this very behaviour. It felt great to save 70% on stuff I knew I would buy anyway at some point during the year.

Let's face it, we can save a lot of money if we shop contrary to the trend.

If at all possible, I tend to buy my winter jackets when there is a heatwave outside. That is when the shops want to get rid of these items, to make space for the summer clothes.

Conversely, I love to buy my summer clothing when there is six feet of snow outside. I know it is not normal to do that, and maybe that is why I like doing it. I love a bargain. I don't think I am alone in loving to buy cheap.

As I said earlier, the world of trading is diametrically opposed to the world *outside* trading. The traits I display as a human being outside my world of trading don't serve me well in the world of trading. This is not just me I am talking about. This is people in general.

Our minds struggle to separate the world of trading from the world of general consumer behaviour. Let's look at the differences.

SUPERMARKET BARGAIN

When I see something in the supermarket that is cheaper than it was before, or that gives me a discount for buying more than one item, I am attracted to buying it. My action is driven by a subconscious drive towards pleasure.

My action is that of a rational consumer who will seek out the cheapest products. The supermarket knows this, and they will tailor their offering to maximise my spending.

My behaviour is driven towards maximising my pleasure – within my budget constraint. When I do so, it gives me a sensation of well-being.

FINANCIAL MARKET BARGAIN

When I see the FTSE Index falling in price during the day, my mind associates falling prices with *value* and *becoming cheap*.

If I act on the impulse, one of two things will happen:

1. My feeling of value is confirmed. The market begins to rise.

2. My feeling of value is not confirmed. The market continues to fall.

My argument is perhaps provocative, but no matter what happens next, I will end up losing – even if I win on the trade.

If I buy with no good reason other than my mind sending me an impulse to say the market is cheap, I will lose if the market continues lower. And why would the market not continue lower? That is the premise of technical analysis. Trends persist. The market suffers from inertia, meaning that whatever it is doing now, the odds are above 50% it will continue to do.

If I buy, and the market begins to rise, I will eventually lose anyway, because I have now taught my mind that it is okay to stick my hand out and catch the proverbial falling knife.

I have created a pattern in my mind that associates buying falling asset prices with pleasure, because I had success with it at some point.

As a side note: when I began taking trading very seriously, I would review my trades when the day was over. I would print out the chart and plot my trades onto it. I realised that some eight out of ten trades were impulse trades. I began to become much more conscious of my trades. As I proceeded down that path, I became more and more profitable. The fewer impulse trades I had, the more money I made, and the more satisfaction I derived from my job.

SELF-ANALYSIS

Through analysis of my trading behaviour – meticulously logging my trades on a chart after the trading day was over – I came to the realisation that I was a prolific *value trader*. I would repeatedly short rising markets. I would repeatedly buy falling markets.

It helps me to remind myself daily that when I am buying, someone else is shorting or getting out of a long position. A significant factor to my trading success, going from being a losing trader to a winning trader, was the realisation that there are no bargains in the financial markets.

SUPERMARKET SUBSTITUTES

When I am shopping for something in the supermarket, and I discover a product has gone up in price, or a product that used to be on offer is no longer on offer, my mind will associate 'this with pain. My mind will direct me towards a substitute. This is perfectly rational human behaviour.

My sister and I laugh about this phenomenon. She lives in Germany and frequently travels with the airline EasyJet from Berlin. She puts it so eloquently, when she says, "I will get up in the middle of the night for a 5 am flight, if it means I can save myself €25."

I think many of us can recognise this trait.

FINANCIAL MARKET SUBSTITUTES

If something has gone up in price in the financial markets, then it means there is demand for it. It may seem expensive, but it merely reflects the equilibrium point between buyers and sellers.

I struggled with this for years. I argued it was expensive, and this faulty view was compounded by the technical indicators I was using.

Indicators like stochastics would suggest a market was *overbought* or *oversold*. Those are other words for *cheap* and *expensive*. It is for this reason I am no longer trading with any kind of technical indicators. My charts are 100% naked.

The perverseness of the financial markets is that it generally makes sense to buy something because it is more expensive today than it was yesterday.

DEALING WITH ADVERSITY

When I experience difficult situations in my life, I will be patient and work on resolving them. Through my work and my resolve, I hope I will be able to solve the problem. I may even use force on the issue or use my authority to solve the problem.

No amount of hard work, resolve or prayer will turn a bad trading position into a good position. Either the market agrees with you or it doesn't. It doesn't matter how rich you are; how big and powerful you are. If the market disagrees, it disagrees.

The market can only hurt you if you let it hurt you. The market will rally. The market will fall. Whether you are on board or not, making money or not, is inconsequential to the market. It knows nothing about you.

When you make money, you make money because you are aligned with the market. The market itself is nothing more than the combined force of all the market players. They, like you, are looking to make money from trading.

Unfortunately, we can't all make money. I came to realise, after years of suffering, that I had to change my relationship – not with the market, but with how I reacted to what the market did.

Much of that process was undoing my life values and beliefs when it came to the trading world. In the normal world, when I don't get my will, I will work hard at convincing the other party to see things my way. I am very persuasive, and I usually get things how I want them.

While that may be a trait that helped me in the real world, it is a trait that was detrimental to my trading performance. The market doesn't care about your position. It doesn't care if you are long or short or on the side lines. The market has no feelings about you or your position.

The essence of my argument is that many of the traits we display as perfectly normal people don't serve us well in the world of trading.

I think all the successful traders I know have gone through a transformation process. Some were gradual. Others talk about a specific situation which acted as a catapult to success.

Some became so disgusted with themselves, they decided that they were going to either follow the rules or quit trading altogether.

THE INNOCENCE OF OBJECTIVE OBSERVATION

A very good friend of mine, Dr David Paul, describes his own transformation in the following story.

> I have a PhD in mechanical engineering. I have worked for De Beers. I invented a mining drill which made me a fortune. I have had my own mining company. So, it is fair to say that I came into the markets with a lot of confidence, and a lot of money at my disposal.

I started investing money in the 1980s. It was easy to make money in the stock market then. All you had to do was buy shares and then sit and wait. While I waited, I started doing programming on the early computers. I eventually created my own share selection software. It was incredibly sophisticated software for its time.

On this particular day in question the software called for the market to rise very strongly. So, at the open of trading I phoned my broker and placed a very large buy order.

And sure enough, the market did what my software had said it would do. It started moving higher. I was naturally happy that the analysis was correct and that I was making money. I held on because the software predicted the rise would continue, only much more strongly.

A short while later, however, the market began to drop. I was naturally a little surprised but knew that it must be just a temporary aberration and a good chance to buy a little more before the market really took off. So, I did. I bought some more. And yet the market continued to drop. And drop. And drop.

I began to get a little worried, so I phoned my broker and all my trading friends to see if there was any reason for this deviation. They too were at a loss to explain why the market was down. Their analysis had suggested the market would rally strongly. All the newsletters suggested that we were in the middle of a major wave three in Elliott Wave Analysis terms, and everything pointed to higher prices.

I felt somewhat better having spoken to my friends and my broker about the situation, and I was sure that this was just an aberration, so I decided to buy a little bit more at these cheaper price levels. The market bounced for a while, and I felt pretty good about having bought some more at what I thought would be the lows of the day.

The market then began to head lower again, and I began to get really concerned, even a little scared. It was quite a big position I had accumulated.

Just then my wife walked into my office to ask what I wanted for dinner that night. She must have sensed that I was distracted or in discomfort, and she walked over to my desk and looked at the trading screen. "Is anything the matter, dear?" she asked. She can be so sweet.

"No, my love, just working. My software says this market should go up." I pointed at the screen. "The software has never been wrong, and I have spoken to the brokers and to my friends, and they all say that this market should be going up, but it is going down."

She looked at the screen with the market and said, "Is this the market you are trading in?"

"Yes," I said. "I really don't understand why it keeps moving lower. I am sure it will move up very soon."

"But it is not moving up right now, is it?" she said.

I got a little impatient with her, and I said, "No dear, but what you don't understand is that the software and the Elliott Wave Count are in agreement, and the market absolutely has to go up."

"Oh well, you are right, I don't know anything about this software or the Elliott thing, but it just doesn't seem to be going up right now, does it?"

I distinctly remember taking a deep breath. I said to the woman I love but who had now begun to irritate me, "No dear, but just as soon as this passes, it will start to go up. It absolutely has to. I think this is just an AB=CD formation. The software says so. The broker says so. My trading friends say so. The Elliott Count says so. There is no way that all these people and my software could be wrong."

"Ok, I am sorry, you are right; I don't understand your software or the Elliott thing or what the broker is talking about. All I see is that this market *right now* is going *down*, isn't it?"

I stopped staring at the screen for a second, and I looked up at my wife. "Could you please repeat what you just said?"

She looked at me puzzled, and said, "Well, I am just saying that *right now*, right at this moment, right here right now, this market is moving down, isn't it?"

And then it hit me like a thunderbolt. I wasn't trading the market. I was trading my opinion. I began to laugh, because I felt for the first time that I knew what had to be done to make money in the market. I understood that the very thing I was trying to avoid was the very thing that was killing me right now. I was trying to avoid losing trades at all cost, and now I was in a trade that was losing me – only because I refused to listen to what the market was trying to tell me.

I realised in that moment that I had to learn to lose in order to win. It was as simple as that. I wasn't trading the market. I was reinforcing my ego through the market.

I picked up the phone, called my broker and sold out all my long positions. Furthermore, I sold a large number of contracts short as well. And sure enough, the market continued – down and down and down.

My trading life changed that day. I no longer paid so much attention to expert theories, and I stopped guessing where the market was going. I started trading the markets. It was a revelation. I started making lots of money. I realised that some of the stuff I had read was outright wrong and detrimental to my trading.

For example, we have all read the axiom of 'buy low and sell high'. I changed that to 'sell low and cover lower' and 'buy high and sell higher'.

SURRENDER

When I asked David to sum up his experience, he said to me:

> Look at your own life. You love to surf. You wait for the waves, and you paddle into their energy flow, and you ride the wave. How is that any different to what we do as traders?

> When you are out there, sitting outside the impact zone, waiting to paddle in, you don't paddle when there are no waves. You are patient. When the right size wave builds ups, you get ready. You are one with the sea. You roll with its flow. You surrender.

To succeed in the markets, we must surrender. Every single individual on planet Earth has a great deal of time, money and value tied up in *what we know*, and it is unthinkable to even consider surrendering all this perceived knowledge.

The purpose of my trading and your trading is not to be proven right and bolster our egos. Our job is to make money. If that means we come to the market with an opinion, and we are proven right, so be it.

If it means we have to change our opinion because the market dictates it, so be it. A more spiritual person than I would perhaps express this as "empty your mind and let the market guide you".

THERE IS A LOT LESS TO TRADING THAN MEETS THE EYE

The fact is that our complicated human minds have a great deal of trouble processing information that is simple. Unless it is complex to the tenth degree, our minds tend to pass it over. We think that something simple can't be profitable.

What is your aim? The simple answer should be to make money. In the past I was so preoccupied with what *should happen*. But to make money we must be focused on what is happening right here, right now.

When I started writing this book, I wanted to keep it practical. I had no interest in trying to pass myself off as a trader therapist or a psychologist, because I am not. I wanted it to show the true nature of what trading is, written by someone who has skin in the game, and who has both scars and medals to show for it.

If the last few pages have been a little too theoretical for your liking, I would like to describe a real-life case study – one that was captured on video (my way of telling you that this is an authentic story) by Round the Clock Trader in July 2019.

I want to explain what I mean by going into the market with an open mind and an empty cup. I bought an index after a double bottom. Everything looked pretty good. I was long from 12,808 and I had bought again at 12,818. Then it happened: the index plummeted. My five-minute chart showed three major lows (I call these *get out* bars, when I am trading against their direction, or *add to* bars, when I am on the right side of them). I was wrong being long.

I got out of my long position and reversed my position to short, relatively early on in the downward spiral of the index. There were some 500 traders attending the event, and what pleased me most about the outcomes was not that I lost on my first trade, or that I won my money back soon after. What pleased me most was that I did not stubbornly hold on to a losing trade, and that I had the mental freedom to move from being long the market to now being short the market.

When I started trading, there was no chance in hell I would have done what I did there. I would have held on and held on to that losing position. "I know I am right," I would have said; except I wasn't, and I wasn't making money.

The most critical point came when my new short position showed a profit which was equal to what I had lost on the long position. My mind desperately wanted me to bring balance to its emotions. What better way to do that than to offset the loss from the first trade? Well, in the words of my greatest trading hero, Charlie DiFrancesca, "Good trading means combatting the emotions that make us human." Let's take a look at how we can do that.

FIGHTING MY HUMANNESS

WHAT IS NORMAL behaviour amongst retail traders? We know that 80–90% of all retail traders engage in the same self-destructive behavioural pattern.

We know that some 90% of traders do not make money consistently trading CFDs or spread betting or in futures markets. It is probably also fair to assume that those 80–90% of traders are intelligent, ambitious, self-motivated human beings, who like to create their own luck and forge their own way in life.

I have never met anyone who started trading because they thought it was the same as playing the lottery. Virtually every person I have ever met who was interested in trading and who wanted to learn more about trading has been a self-starter, entrepreneur, or student at an institution of further education.

Therefore, it's a fallacy to say trading attracts the wrong kind of people. It attracts the right kind of people. It attracts those who have a chance of succeeding at it.

I think it attracts the kind of people who are not fooled by the get-rich-quick schemes. I doubt many traders buy lottery tickets, purely on account of the odds being rubbish, and traders understanding that all too well.

Nevertheless, something is wrong.

Something is wrong when 90% of people fail. In the following table I have identified a handful of behavioural patterns that I think are detrimental to traders. The most frequently observed behaviour is the inability to take a loss.

What is the reason for not taking a loss? I argue there is one reason we tell ourselves, and then there is another, real reason. The real reason is always the same.

Action	Conscious Reason	Subconscious Reason
1. I am letting my loss run	I am hoping	Avoid pain
2. I am letting my loss run	Indicator/Fib/etc., says so	Avoid pain
3. I am taking my profits	You can't go broke taking a profit	Avoid pain
4. I am winning, so I am reducing my stake	I want to take it easy now	Avoid pain
5. I am losing, so I am increasing my stake	I am trying to get back to where I was	Get rid of pain
6. I made my points for today, so I stop	I am afraid to lose what I made	Avoid pain
7. I am trading without real conviction	I am bored/scared of missing out	Avoid pain of boredom or pain of missing out

Hope features high on the list of reasons. As the saying goes, hope dies last. Our minds seem ill equipped to engage in risk management. Our minds have one primary objective: to protect us against perceived or real pain.

During the process of running an open position that is producing a loss, our subconscious mind is telling our conscious mind to keep the position open. It will mask this message as well as it can, in order to protect the ego, which is more fragile than the state of your trading account.

If this sounds too airy-fairy, on account of the use of words like *ego* and *subconscious*, let's explore the same argument using a different language.

AVOIDING PAIN

As long as a losing position is open, there is hope that the position will turn positive. The moment you close the position, and you crystallise the loss, the pain of the loss becomes real.

I accept there are many permutations to the situation of handling a losing trade. Some will argue that the very act of closing a losing trade is the point when you can stop agonising over the open loss and open yourself up to other trade options. I personally agree with this argument. When I have a losing position and I no longer believe in it, the worst I can do to myself and my psyche is to begin to hope. I don't feel free in my thinking and in my market perspective when an open losing position is beaming at me on my open position monitor. When I close the position, I feel free again, and I am opening myself up to taking in market information from an opportunistic frame of mind.

However, my primary argument is that the reason we are hoping has little to do with hope itself and everything to do with avoiding pain.

How many times did I see clients sit on losing positions for ages? I saw them deposit more money every time their losing position received a margin call. A margin call is when the broker demands more money to keep your position open. They just didn't want to take the loss.

To compound my confusion, how many times did I see the position come good again, and the client close the position as soon as it did? I saw it frequently. They didn't hold on to the position because they believed in the position. They held on to the position because they could not stand being wrong.

The moment they were relieved of their pain of the losing position, they got out – for nothing. They were so relieved to have avoided the pain of being wrong that they completely ignored the fact that the market was now actually agreeing with them.

They weren't trading the financial market. They were trading their emotions, responding to how they felt. When they felt relief that the position had come good again, they now associated a tremendous amount of pain with the thought of having to relive this anxiety once more.

As a result of this association, they closed the position. They felt relieved at the thought of not having to go through this anxiety again.

If you are taking your profits early under the excuse that 'you can't go broke taking a profit', you are reacting to your mind warning you against future pain.

If you are on a winning streak, and you reduce your stake size, you are essentially anticipating the pain of losing some of your gains. You are now rationalising your way to avoid the pain, even though nothing painful has actually happened.

I want to reiterate the last paragraph. If you are in doubt whether you are trading from an opportunistic frame of mind or a fear-based frame of mind, then answer this simple question: when you are winning, are you increasing your trading size or decreasing your trading size?

You see, the vast majority of traders will *decrease* their trading size when things are going well, because they are afraid their winning streak will eventually run out. The flip side to that coin is that they might even increase their trading size during a trading slump, so they can win back the lost money.

As Greg De Riba, an S&P 500 pit trader of superior quality, said in the movie *Floored*: "99% still don't get it – when they win, they start betting less. Bet more!"

Perceived pain or real pain matters not to the subconscious. It will be treated with the same response and the same emotions.

When the pain is real, i.e., real pain has manifested itself in body and mind because of a trading loss, there is no end to the lengths our ego will go to in its efforts to make the money back. This is the primary driver behind the argument of 'when wrong, double up'.

During a losing streak we tell ourselves that we are ever so close to winning again, so the natural conclusion must be to double up in order to regain what has been lost.

The real (subconscious) reason for doubling up on a losing trade is to attempt to get rid of the pain. Now we are not trying to avoid pain; we are dealing with existing pain, and we are trying to get back to that state of equilibrium where we were pain free.

ACT WITHOUT FEAR

You learn a lot from observing millions of trades. If you want to stand a genuine chance of making money as a trader from the financial markets, I believe with every string of DNA within me, with every fibre in my body, that you need to change the way you think about fear and pain and hope.

William Blake said that "He who desires, but acts not, breeds pestilence". I have worked tirelessly towards being able to act without fear and hesitation. The true measure of your growth as a human being is not what you know, but rather what you do with the things you know.

What do I mean by that?

Have you ever seen a chart pattern, and your first impulse was to buy or sell short, but then – without warning – the very next thought was one of fear? It was a thought you had no control over. It just exploded into the forefront of your mind.

I have experienced that at times in my career. When it happens, I know I need to reset somehow. Maybe I need to meditate. Maybe I need to sleep. Maybe I need to eat or go for a walk. I know that something is blocking me, and I need to resolve it.

My free creative mind instructed me to do something, but my fear instinct immediately cautioned me not to follow through, because I might lose.

It doesn't really matter whether you were right not to trade, or whether the position would have lost you money or made you money. Those are afterthoughts (rationalisations or justifications). We can file those under *anecdotal evidence*, or evidence that has no merit. We all have an uncle who smoked until he was 90 with no negative effects – anecdotal evidence – but that does not justify the argument for smoking.

If my free mind argues for a position, and my fear mind argues about the consequences of failing on that trade, then I am essentially arguing with myself. The posh term for this phenomenon is *cognitive dissonance*.

My trades need to flow from a point of freedom of expression. Trades conducted from a perspective of fear or greed will not lead to good decision making.

My advice: stop trading and start contemplating. What is going on? When I experience cognitive dissonance, it is for one or both of the following reasons:

1. I have trading fatigue (or physical fatigue – ever heard the saying 'fatigue makes cowards of us all'?).

2. I haven't done my preparation well enough.

HOW DOES SHE DANCE?

Have you ever seen a market that was in freefall, and you were reluctant to sell short because you were afraid you might lose? My basic aim with this book is *not* to rid you of these fears. Fear will always be part of our lives. My aim is to make you understand why you feel that fear and how to process it, so you can take the trade.

I accept that I am a human ruled by emotions. I understand that I can't escape emotions, and nor should I try to escape them. Rather I want to help you understand your fear, why it is there, and how to become friends with it.

Earlier in the book I wrote about Philippe Petit, the man who walked across a wire suspended between the Twin Towers. He is afraid of spiders. Yes, it sounds silly, doesn't it? His approach to dealing with fear is worth repeating.

He would do everything in his power to understand the nature of his fear of spiders. He would study spiders. He would learn everything there was to know about spiders. Through his study he would come to appreciate the nature of his fear.

How does that translate into the world of trading? Let's take a practical example. I am trading the FTSE 100 Index. My stake size is around £300 a point for a starter position. Now I have to find the best entry points and the best exit points.

But what do I do if I am afraid? What do I do if I am scared to place my trades because I am not sure what the market is capable of doing?

The greater understanding you have of your opponent, the better you are able to understand what she is doing. I use the word *opponent* here, but really, the market, she is my friend. I want to dance with her. But I am afraid of making a fool of myself. So, I study her moves.

I haven't seen other traders do what I do, so I argue this is a novel way of analysing the markets. Whether it is a new approach or not doesn't matter. What matters is that I get a sense of what my dancing partner is capable of doing. What can I expect from her price behaviour? Is it erratic? Is it smooth?

Observe the chart in Figure 9.

We are all chart experts after the fact. However, studying past pricing behaviour gives me a strong indication of what I can expect for the

Figure 9

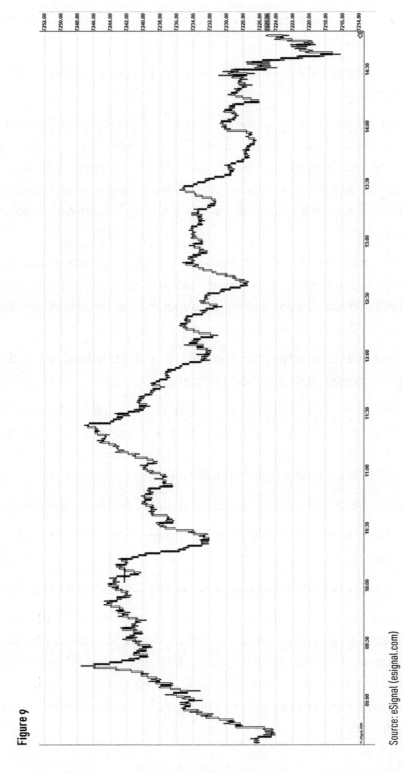

Source: eSignal (esignal.com)

trading day. You may see a market that initially rallies, makes a double top, and then declines.

Let me show you the chart in Figure 9 from another vantage point – see Figure 10.

As part of my quest to trade without fear, I break down the chart into its smallest components. I see the first wave up is 24 points. I see the retracement is 9 points down. I see an attempt to make new highs, but it only rallies 6 points. I see a deeper retracement of 12 points. I see an 8-point rally, a 3-point retracement and another 11-point rally.

The retracements lower are between 9 and 12 points, with the exception of one move of 17 points. You may argue that this is *great* (said with sarcasm), if you had known about it *before* the trading session started. Well, you did. Let me show you the day before, in Figure 11.

The retracements lower are between 7 and 12 points, with the exception of one move that was 14 points.

My approach to a non-fearful trading style is a combination of emotional discipline, mental warm-up, and knowledge of what the market can do. While these two trading days are different in outcome, their behaviour is not altogether different.

I would go into the trading day armed with the following knowledge:

1. Deep retracements and outright moves tend to be around 10 points.

2. Small retracements against a strong trend are around 3–7 points.

Knowing this, combined with an understanding of basic price patterns, I can develop an entry strategy aimed at risking as little as possible. For example, on the previous chart, after the market has pushed higher for a move of +11, I wait to buy a retracement. I know that most retracements are around 7 to 12 points, with the last three of them being 8, 7 and 10.

Figure 10

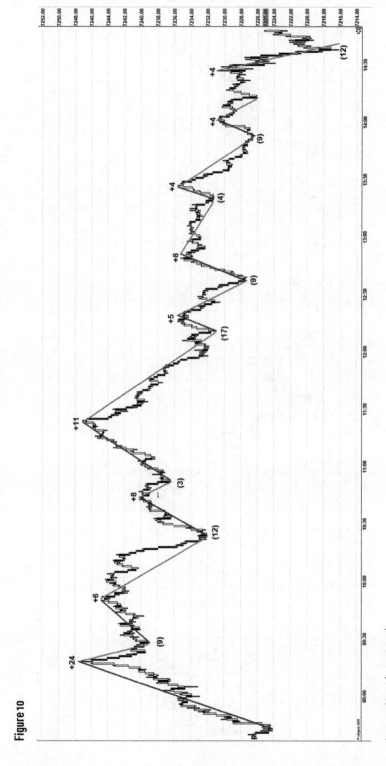

Source: eSignal (esignal.com)

Figure 11

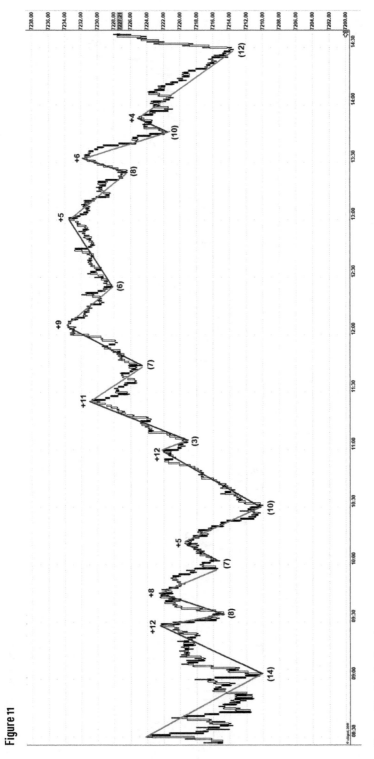

Source: eSignal (esignal.com)

So now I am looking to buy. Say I buy at the point where the market has retraced –7 points; I may be fearful that the market will move against me. My knowledge of the immediate past suggests that the market is unlikely to move more than –12 points in a retracement. I therefore place my stop-loss at an appropriate distance away, based on the past behaviour.

The discipline to wait for the right entry, combined with the knowledge of past price behaviour, will set you apart from the majority of traders. They are unlikely to have done the same level of preparation.

Through your preparation (and I admit, I speak for myself now), you are working through the issues your *fear mind* can throw at you. Your fear mind might say "What if I lose?" If it does, the answer is that if the market moves beyond –12 points your position is probably wrong, and your stop-loss will handle your exit.

When I lend a helping hand to struggling traders via my Telegram channel, the first thing I ask them is do they write down their trades? By that I don't mean write the particular trade entry on a piece of paper. I mean, do they plot their trade entries on a chart once the trading day is over?

I have included a couple of examples from my own trading diary to serve as a visual reference guide. See Figures 12 and 13. I use these to warm up in the morning ahead of the trading day. I have selected random files from my old trading days, and I will relive those moments, both the terrible ones – to get me fired up on *how not to trade today* – as well at the good ones for inspiration.

By observing my past behaviour, I am able to reinforce my good points while being mindful of my weak points. I will observe the disastrous consequences of my hasty trading decisions and my impulses. I will observe trades where I didn't let my profits run. I will in essence torment myself by looking at my bad trades because I know this will act as a positive catalyst.

Figure 12

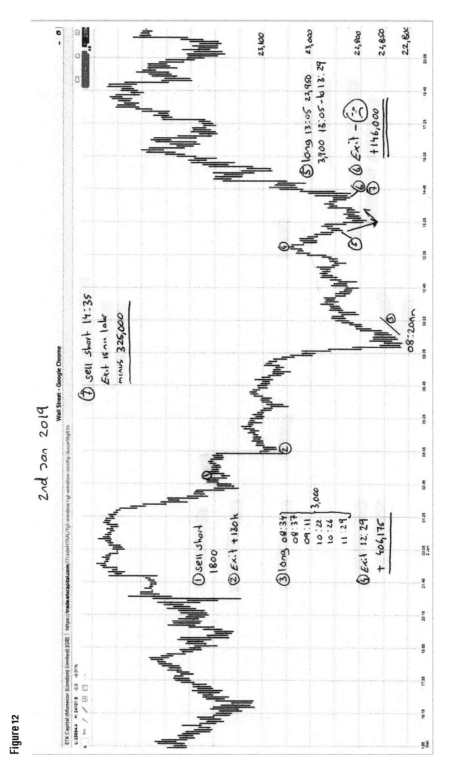

Figure 13

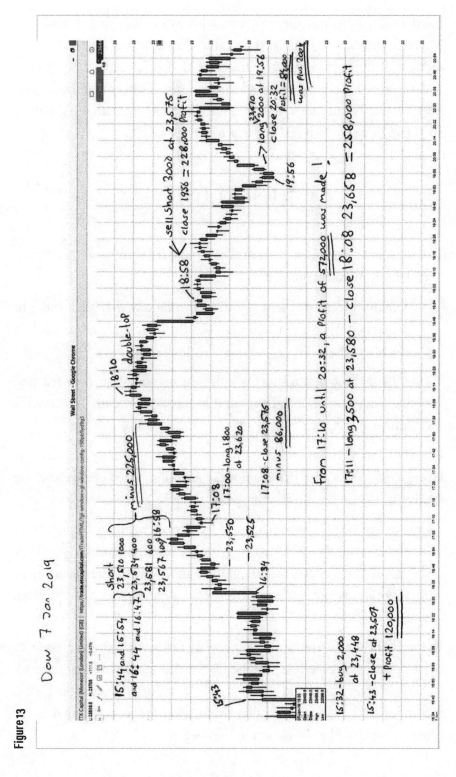

Dow 7 Jan 2019

Incidentally, I am not the only one who works like that. I read that Michael Jordan and Cristiano Ronaldo thrive on negative talk about them and their performance. They take that on board, and it acts as fuel to propel them to greater achievements. Unfortunately, no one writes about Tom Hougaard and his trading, so I recreate the situation by putting myself through my past bad trades.

NOT ALONE

The disastrous, impulsive patterns I saw most frequently on the trading floor fell into two categories:

1. Clients executed a long position in markets that they thought looked cheap. More often than not they bought into established downtrends.

2. Clients executed a short position in markets that they felt had rallied by too much. To them it looked as if the market couldn't move any higher.

I don't blame you if you think I am making this up. Surely, traders can't be engaged in this kind of behaviour in an enlightened era like the one we live in, where information flows so freely?

To prove my point, I went to the IG Client Sentiment Report from 26 October 2021. IG Markets is a broker that has been around for some time. Their client base is global, and as such their sentiment report represents the trade positions of a large segment of the retail trading community.

Before I show you the sentiment report for stock indices, I want to tell you that as I type this, on the day of the sentiment report, stock indices all over the world made *fresh new all-time highs*. The FTSE 100 Index in the UK traded at levels not seen for years. In the US the Dow Index traded at levels *never* seen before.

So, you would imagine that if my observations were inaccurate, the bias on the sentiment report would call for people being *bullish* the market.

You would be wrong. Sadly, I was right about traders' behaviour. 71.39% of all Dow Index positions were short positions – on a day when the Dow made fresh new all-time highs. Things were not much better for the DAX Index or the FTSE Index.

Symbol	Net-Long (%)	Net-Short (%)
Germany 30	37.04	62.96
FTSE 100	30.60	69.40
US 500	39.85	60.15
Wall Street	28.61	71.39

This is why the 90% lose. We don't see the market for what it is. We see it as we are. A chart is only as illuminating as our ability to keep out preconceived ideas of the direction of the market.

We are not losing money over time because we don't know enough about technical analysis or the markets as a whole. We lose money because we refuse to accept what is right in front of us.

My basic premise is that people:

1. think the wrong way before they get into a trade, and

2. think the wrong way when they are in a trade.

It reminds me of the late Mark Douglas, a phenomenal light in the trading industry and an inspiration to thousands of people, when he said that good traders "think differently from everyone else" at the start of his book *Trading in the Zone*.

I have coined my own phrase. I argue that people are fearful when they should be hopeful, and they are hopeful when they should be fearful. I would like to illustrate that by use of an example.

Imagine you have bought German DAX Index at 15,510 and the market is now trading up at 15,525. Instead of thinking that the market may be on a tear – and may go on to offer you many more points – you begin to fear that the points you have already earned will be taken away from you.

Hence my saying: you should be hopeful in a situation like this, but instead you are fearful. You are afraid that the points will be taken away from you. You are not thinking about how many points this position may end up making you. Your focus is on fear rather than opportunity.

The opposite holds true when you are in a losing position. You are now hoping that the market will turn around. Your sole objective is to get rid of your pain, and instead of being afraid that you're going to lose even more, you now hope that you can reach a position in which you will lose less. Every tick in your favour is celebrated. Every tick against you is ignored.

If you want to trade well, you need to turn this on its head. You need to teach your brain to be hopeful (about profits) when it is wrongly fearful (about losing the profits). You need to teach your brain to be fearful (about losses) when it is mistakenly hopeful (about the position turning positive).

It starts with being mindful of this behaviour. Perhaps a conversation with a student of mine can further clarify what I am talking about.

CONVERSATION WITH A STUDENT

In the following conversation, my student and I are discussing a long position I have running in Sterling Dollar.

Student: It feels like gambling.

Tom: Please explain.

Student: Well, I have 40 pips in profit, but you will not let me take the profit.

Tom: I won't stop you from taking the profit, but if you ask for my opinion, you should let the position run. You might want to consider the following scenarios, and then ask yourself how you would feel in each case:

1. Run position and you get stopped out for nothing.

2. Run position and it explodes higher.

3. Close position and it explodes higher.

4. Close position and it reverses.

Student: I think it is best to close the position and secure the profits, rather than risk that the market will take the profits away from me.

Tom: How would you then feel if the market exploded higher – in your favour?

Student: I would be disappointed, but I could always jump back in again.

Tom: If you jumped back in, you would have to pay commission again or at least the spread, and you would have missed the explosive move. The only way you would profit from the explosive move is if you were already in the move.

Student: Yes, but at least I would be playing for momentum to continue.

Tom: That is true, but you are already in a position where the momentum is on your side.

Student: I guess I just don't want to see my profits disappear.

And there you have it – in a nutshell. People are hopeful when they are losing money. They are fearful when they are making money. I believe this is how the 90% think. It is the reason why – in a study of 25,000 traders – they won more often than they lost, but they lost 66% more on their average loss than they gained on their average win.

When the trader is confronted with a loss, they hope it will turn around. The operative word here is *hope*. When they are confronted with a profitable position, they are afraid the profit will disappear. The operative word in this scenario is *fear*.

My student naïvely thought he could jump back in again, but he would undoubtedly have had to do so at a worse price than the exit price of his profitable position.

So, the trader holds onto the position until a point at which the pain finally becomes too much, then closes the position. Unfortunately, this threshold tends to be further down the road than the threshold of hope.

This is what you need to focus on.

This is what you need to work on constantly to change your pattern. I will not state whether it will be easy to do or difficult to do. It just is. There is no point in going any further in speculation if you can't get yourself to do what you must do, even though it feels uncomfortable.

You must be aware that in trading we tend to chase hope a lot further down the road of misery than we are prepared to follow the road of opportunity. It is just the way we are put together. You must be aware of this and have a plan for combatting your natural behaviour.

However, I must warn you. Your mind is like a muscle. This is not a one-off quick fix any more than doing 100 push-ups once will make you look like Captain America for the rest of your life.

Atrophy is not just something that happens to bodies. It also affects our minds. You need to strengthen that mind of yours through repetition. I present my own training regime at the end of the book, although I am actually describing it piece by piece as we move through the book.

THE NOT-SO-NORMAL BEHAVIOUR

What is *not-so-normal behaviour*? Well, firstly, I am all too aware of the shortcomings most people display when they are trading: running a loss, cutting short the profitable positions, over-trading, trading for excitement and entertainment.

But this is already known to most – if not all – people, so the not-so-normal behaviour goes somewhat beyond that. It is very rare that we ask ourselves why we do what we do. Why do I trade when I do? Why do I take profits when I do?

I think it's time to bring in the words of a relatively unknown trader (but one who was hugely respected by his peers). He was a pit trader at the Chicago Board of Trade (CBOT), and his name was Charlie DiFrancesca, also known as 'Charlie D'.

MY HERO

Charlie DiFrancesca arrived at the floor of the CBOT with a dream and a small account. He had a background in competitive college football – American style – but otherwise there was nothing about this guy that would indicate he would go on to become the biggest trader in the US Treasury bond pit in Chicago.

He had a rough start. He barely traded in the first six months on the floor. He just stood there and observed. Then one afternoon something clicked, and he traded up a storm for two hours, making himself $5,000. From then onwards there was no stopping Charlie D. He became a legend in the trading pit until his untimely death.

In William D. Falloon's biography of Charlie D., the great trader says:

The time you know you've become a good trader is that first day you were able to win by holding and adding to a winning position. There are many people here (in the trading pit) that have traded for a long time, and who have never added to a winner.

Adding to winning trades is an absolute key trait of the successful trader. It reinforces correct behaviour. It serves as an antidote to the temptation of wanting to take profit. When I am in a profitable position, I have trained my mind to ask, "How can I make my position bigger?" rather than dwelling on the idea of taking profits.

Charlie D. goes on to talk about his own mentor, Everett Klipp, who taught him about correct trading:

> Unfortunately, it's only human nature to want to cut your winning trades. Say I am long at 6, and the market goes 7 bid, our mind instantly thinks *get me out with a profit*. That's human nature. It is also human nature to ride the losses. I am stuck. I won't close. I will wait.

ADDING EPIPHANY

In 2007 I met a person who was going to radically change my way of trading. It all came about by chance. I had come back from a lunch break and a colleague of mine returned from a meeting with an educational company. This educational company taught technical analysis and they were pitching their products to my colleague, who happened to be the head of marketing.

What you need to know about my colleague is that he was the most obnoxious East End London guy you could possibly imagine. He was brash, obnoxious (I know, I said that twice), and arrogant, and no one could tell him anything he didn't already know.

Yet somehow this educational company had gotten his attention. He spoke glowingly about a gentleman called Dr David Paul, who had taken him through some basic technical analysis.

He showed me the technical analysis, and it *was* basic. Yet there was something about the course material, which I had been given a copy of, that told me that I needed to engage in a conversation with this gentleman.

It turned out that Dr David Paul had a two-day trading course coming up in Johannesburg. So a few days later I booked myself onto a flight. It was one of the only times I have ever participated in formal training on the topic of technical analysis.

I have mentioned him before, but I'll describe him a little more now. There is something incredibly humble about Dr David Paul, despite everything he has accomplished. He has a PhD in mechanical engineering. He used his immense abilities to invent a drill for miners in South Africa. This was no ordinary drill. It was the kind that sucks gas out of the ground as it drills, and thus saves lives by more or less eradicating the occurrence of explosions.

David Paul spent much of his time investing and trading. He made himself a wealthy man. On the second day of the course David said something that would change my perspective on trading.

He said something along the lines of this: "When you are in a winning position, instead of thinking where to get out, why don't you think about where to get in more?"

He basically told me to turn everything upside down. Most traders with a profit will begin to contemplate where to take half the profit. Next, they will begin to contemplate where to take the next half of the profit.

David argued that this was what the 90% would do. He didn't use those exact words, but he did argue that if you want to make money trading, you need to do that which the majority finds difficult to do.

The first time you try it, you may fall flat on your face. That is to be expected, but the next time it might be a little easier, and the next time a little easier again.

DO WHAT IS HARD

David was essentially arguing that when you are in a winning position you should put pressure on your position. The argument for doing so was something he himself had observed when the market really began to trend.

I have tried to put a different spin on his words. When you want what you want more than you fear what you want, you will have it. You want profits in your trading. You probably have a good instinct about trading. You probably also realise by now that it is your thinking that causes your problems, rather than your knowledge about the financial markets.

If the 90% of traders are engaged with taking half profits and letting the other half run, maybe the right thing to do is to double up on your position, or perhaps conservatively add a little to the position, when everyone else is taking half the profits. At least this is what I read between the lines, as I sat in that hotel conference room in Johannesburg.

When the workshop was over I walked across the street and locked myself into my hotel room. I sat down and waited. The Dow Index was trending. I waited for a retracement. Then I waited for a five-minute bar to close above the high of the prior five-minute bar.

Then I bought. Ten minutes later I added to my first position. Twenty minutes later I closed at a double top. It was the most satisfying trading moment in my life. A whole new world had opened up to me.

Depending on your experience level, you may or may not be able to answer this question: why is it easier to add to a losing position than a winning position? I have wondered about that myself many times.

You decide that you want to buy the DAX at 12,325. The market then moves down to 12,315 and you are tempted to add to the position.

Why?

Why is it easier to add to a losing position than to a winning position?

Well, for starters, you would have loved to have bought at 12,315 rather than 12,325 because you would have gotten a better entry price. Therefore, buying again at 12,315 makes sense from an economics point of view. That is plain simple logic.

There is a chance that you have a stop-loss in mind, and there is a chance that you have a target in mind. Now you have an opportunity to have the same stop-loss as before, but you have 10 points less risk, and you have more profit potential.

You have also created a better average price, so the market has to move fewer points in your favour before you are at breakeven.

Simple and logical – something our minds love.

However, you will now also have added to your position exposure, and the market has told you that you are wrong, at least right now. It was easy to do the wrong thing because we attach a *value* to the market. When the market gives an opportunity to increase the value of our trade, it will seem compelling to us.

So why is it difficult to add to a winning trade?

If I bought at 12,325, and the market is moving in my favour, I am relieved. Now other emotions will enter the consciousness. There will be greed. You want to make more. There will be fear. You want to protect what you have made.

When the market reaches 12,345, you will be thinking that if you buy more now, you have increased your average price to 12,335. It means that the market will only have to move 10 points against you before your position will be at breakeven, rather than in profit.

The key point here is: what is your mind dwelling on?

When we add to a losing position, we decide to dwell on the potential for bigger profits. We decide not to dwell on the fact that the market is telling us we are wrong. We decide not to dwell on the fact we have just doubled our risk.

When we add to a winning position, we decide to dwell on the fact that the market may take our profits away, because we have now decreased our average price. We decide not to dwell on the fact that the market is corroborating with us.

Put simply, the market disagrees with us, but we have faith that the market is wrong, and we add to a losing position; *or* the market agrees with us by showing a profit, but we doubt the market is right, so we don't add to our winning position.

It doesn't quite make sense, does it? And yet, this is what the majority of traders are doing all the time. Adding to a winning position can be uncomfortable to begin with. No one is saying you have to double up on your trading size the first time you add to a winning position. You could add just a little bit.

ADDING STRATEGIES

There are two ways you can add to your winning trades. You can use a same-size principle, by which you keep adding the same size. Say you buy ten lots to begin with, and then you add ten more lots at a higher price, and so on.

That is a risky way of trading. Instead you could use a second principle, by which your first position is the biggest position, and subsequent positions are smaller. So your first position might be ten lots, but the subsequent positions might be five lots.

When I trade, I pretty much always use the same-size principle, but I urge you to use the second principle until you are comfortable with adding to winning trades.

BUILDING NEW PATHWAYS

The purpose of adding to winning trades is at its heart an attempt to fight your *normal* human behaviour. In the beginning it is not about adding to your profitability. That will come later. The purpose is to stop you from taking *half profits*.

By adding to the winning trade, by thinking, "How can I make more when I am right?" rather than thinking, "Where should I take profit?" you are building a new way of thinking about trading.

Do you remember what Mark Douglas said in the opening lines of *Trading in the Zone*? In trading, consistent winners "think differently from everyone else". When you start to think, "Where can I add to my winning trades?" you are beginning to think differently. From then onwards, it becomes a matter of habit. You have built a new neurological pathway in your mind, or at least taken meaningful steps in the right direction.

CONTROLLING RISK

How do you control risk when you add to winning trades? This is a question I am often asked. The answer is the same whether you are adding to a winning or a losing trade: you place a stop-loss.

Some who receive this answer will say, "But if I get stopped out on an add-on on a profitable trade, then I will have lost profits from the original trade as well."

Yes, that is true; but isn't it better to get stopped out of a trade where you have some profits to cushion your loss, rather than having added to a losing trade, where you are now feeling the full force of the loss? At least when you add to a winning trade, the market is currently agreeing with you.

I have just bought the Dow at 26,629. My stop-loss is 26,590. The Dow has already rallied from a base of 26,569, so I might be a little late to the party, but that doesn't bother me.

Many a good trade has been missed by those arriving too late to the party. As long as I have a stop-loss in place, I am fine to join a momentum move, even one that has been moving for a while.

The Dow prints 26,649, and I buy once more. I am adding to my winning position. Now my stop-loss on the first position I bought has been moved to reflect the fact that I have taken on more risk. My first stop-loss is now at 26,629. The stop-loss on my second position is also 26,629.

At this point, two things can happen. Ideally, the market will carry on moving higher, and every point move is now making me twice as much as if I had only one position.

The less appealing alternative is that the market moves against me, and I will get stopped out of the first position at breakeven, and I will lose 20 points on the second position.

There is no magic to it. It is a philosophy, and it is born out of a desire to *not* be normal. The normal thing to do is to close half your position and let the other half run.

Why would you do that? Why would you have the market agree with you, but you only ride it with half a stake?

That is what the 90% are doing, and I don't want to do what the 90% are doing, no matter how logical it may seem. They are wrong over time, and I want to be right over time!

It is such a crucial point I am attempting to get across to you, right here and right now. I don't know what is going to happen over the course of one trade. Anything can happen. However, I do know what will happen – statistically speaking – over the course of 100 trades.

Over the course of one trade, you may win, or you may lose. Over the course of one coin flip, you may get a *head* or you may get a *tail*, and you may get five tails in a row, but you will still end up – statistically speaking – with a 50/50 outcome when you throw the coin 100 times.

The same applies to trades. You may be on a hot run, and have nothing but winning trades on your screen, but over time it will even itself out. Therefore, it is vitally important you don't think too much about the outcome of one trade, but rather the outcome of 100 trades.

The outcome of one trade is random. The outcome of 100 trades is predictable. It is for this reason that our behaviour needs to be the same for every trade we execute, whether we like it or not. By applying the same correct behaviour to every trade, we are virtually guaranteed to be profitable.

What is the correct behaviour? Well, why don't we observe what everyone else is doing, and then do the opposite of what they are doing?

The basic premise is that the majority of people who trade end up losing money. That is our starting point. Now we observe what those people do. I have been doing that for ten years. Here is what I observed:

1. THEY DON'T ADD TO WINNERS

They don't add to winning trades. So, to be profitable, add to winning trades, whether you add a little or you double up. Start slowly, add a little.

2. THEY DON'T USE A STOP-LOSS

They don't like to use a stop-loss, because that would crystallise the pain of the loss. As long as the position is open, there is hope. So, to be profitable over time, use a stop-loss. Use a stop-loss on your first position and on subsequent positions.

3. THEY ADD TO LOSING TRADES

We all love a bargain at the local supermarket, don't we? And by all means, continue to shop for bargains at the local supermarket; but do not do it in the financial markets by buying more, just because you can buy it at a cheaper price than the first time you bought it.

While you may get lucky from time to time, this is one of the main traits of losing traders. Remember, we are focused on establishing the behaviour that will ensure we will be profitable over time.

4. THEY TAKE HALF PROFITS

This one is going to be tough to argue, so bear with me. I know so many traders – even people who have traded for decades longer than I have – who advocate taking half profits. Their thinking goes along this pathway:

I will risk 20 points.

I will take half profits at 20 points and move stop-loss on the other half to breakeven.

I will take the other half profit at 40 points.

It sounds so compelling. You close half the position, so if the market turns around, at least you will have made 20 points on half the position. I can understand the thinking behind it.

The problem I have with this strategy is that it never gives you the home-run trades that you need to sustain yourself in this business. You will never be on board the big moves because you have always limited yourself.

I have two fundamental arguments against taking half profits:

1. The market agrees with you. Let it ride.

2. Since I don't believe in the *risk-to-reward* argument, because no human being can know in advance what their *reward* will be without limiting themselves, I don't believe that taking half profits is the right way to trade.

RISK TO REWARD

Did I just say that I don't believe in the whole risk-to-reward argument? Yes, that is correct. I do not. I believe in defining my risk. I don't believe in defining my reward.

When I am about to execute a trade, there is *only* one variable I have meaningful control over: how much money/points/pips will I risk on this trade?

Anything else is pure guess work. How much I will make will depend on the market. It will not depend on me, unless I put a limit on my profits. A very wise old trader once told me that losers spend their time thinking how much they will make, while winners spend their time thinking about how much they will lose.

The only variable I am in control of, as a *point-and-click trader* (as opposed to one who uses an algorithm), is how much I can lose on a trade. Observing hundreds of millions of trades over a decade, executed by an army of well-meaning traders doing their best to make a profit, I have come to the conclusion that setting a limit on your profits is not the way forward.

If I buy the FTSE 100 Index at 7,240 with a stop-loss at 7,235, and a *take-profit* target at 7,250, I am sure I will be happy if the FTSE goes to 7,250 and reverses back down again. However, how will I feel if the FTSE moves to 7,260, or 7,270, or higher?

Of course, there are exceptions to this rule. I may genuinely want to get out at 7,250 because I feel there is overhead resistance at this area. It may even be an area where I would want to sell short the market. I may also put in a take-profit order at 7,250 because I may not be able to follow the market as closely on this particular trade.

But generally, I do not work with targets because a target will limit my profit, particularly on days where the market is in a runaway mode. With this in mind, I would like to show you an example of a decision I made, and how it ended up costing me dearly.

HOW NOT TO DO IT

The DAX gapped up, as shown in Figure 14. I know from statistics that 48% of all gaps get filled on the same day they occur. Considering that 90% of daily highs and lows occur in the first hour and a half of the trading day, I felt reasonably good about shorting the DAX on the low bar, indicated by the arrow. The stop-loss was close to the high of the day. The risk was 35 DAX points.

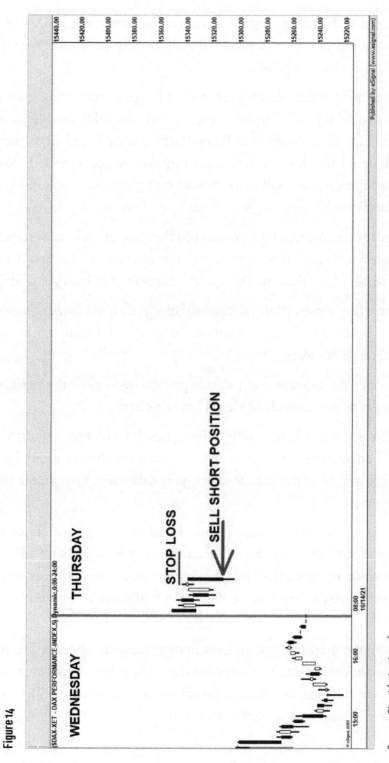

Figure 14

Source: eSignal (esignal.com)

As shown in Figure 15, instead of continuing lower, the DAX Index consolidates and moves higher, and it eventually takes out my stop-loss. I am now at –35 points.

The previous pattern does suggest higher prices to come. Yes, it looks like a double top sell; but on a gap up day, the odds are higher of continuation than of a reversal. Remember the saying, "In bull markets, resistance is often broken, and in bear markets support rarely holds." Well, you can replace bull markets with bull trends, and bear markets with bear trends.

In Figure 16, I execute a long position on the close of the bar, as it closes above my stop-loss. It is in reality a *stop and reverse* situation. I am stopped out of my short position, and as a result of it, I am going long.

The market moves into a consolidation, and eventually breaks higher. I add to my long position, as show in Figure 17. So far everything looks okay.

Then I make a mistake. I am at this point able to close the position with a profit that exceeds the loss I made earlier.

Do you see what I am doing wrong now? I am not trading the chart. I am trading my account. I am trading my state of mind. I am trying to get rid of the pain from my previous trade. You can see this in Figure 18.

Much to my disappointment, I admit I close my long position for no other reason than being able to offset the prior loss. I talk myself out of the position rather than just moving my stop-loss higher. It is not until my review of my trading day that I really come to realise what I have done.

For now the market is not entirely in disagreement with me. For the next two hours the market trades sideways. The longer a market moves from a trending market into a sideways market, the less the prior trend matters. At least that is what I tell myself.

Figure 15

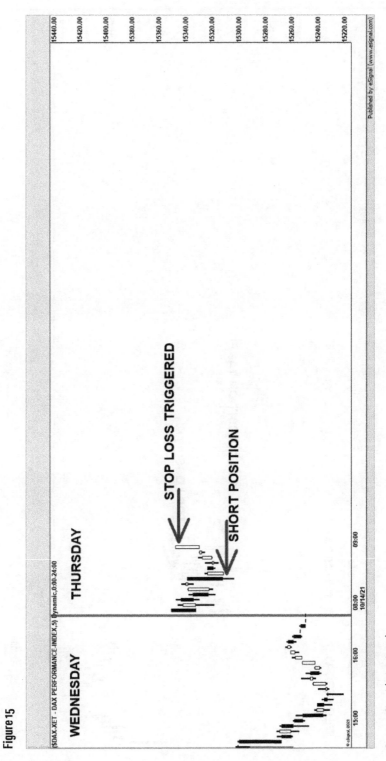

Source: eSignal (esignal.com)

Figure 16

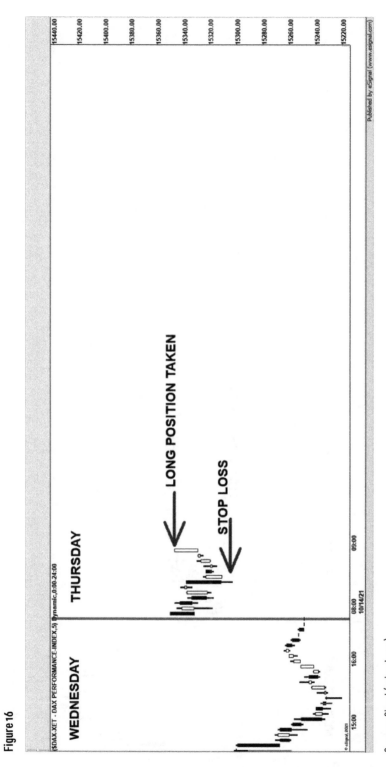

Source: eSignal (esignal.com)

Figure 17

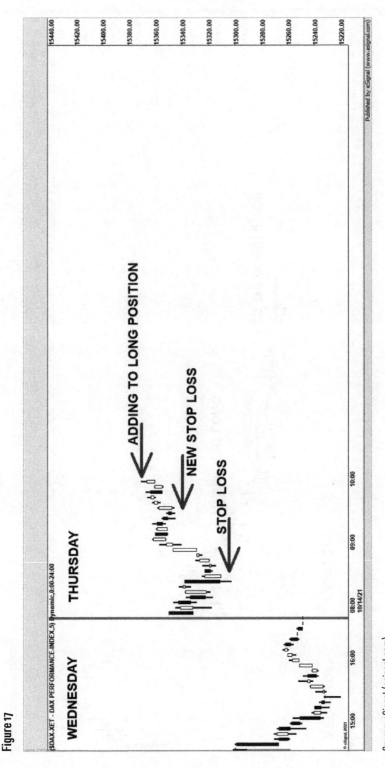

Source: eSignal (esignal.com)

Figure 18

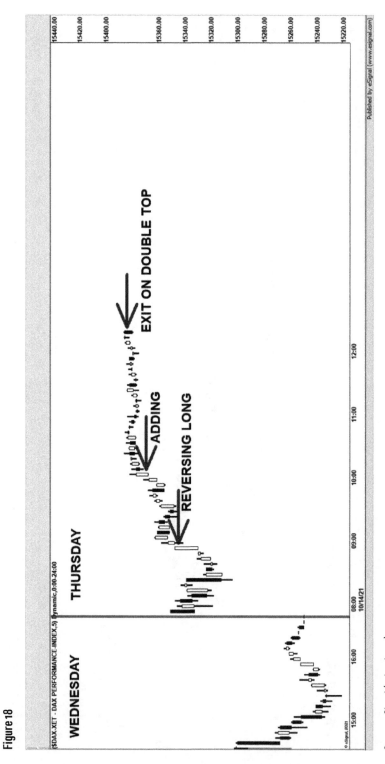

Source: eSignal (esignal.com)

Then as the US markets opens the DAX Index moves higher, and I am not on board. You may not yet see the subtle point I am making here, so let me point it out to you.

I do not belong to the brigade of traders who believe that "you can't go broke taking a profit." I do think you can go broke taking a profit, if it means you never have really big profit days because you are unable to let profits run.

Simple as that!

Figure 19 shows what happened after my exit. While I don't insist on perfect trading, I review my trades religiously to pick up on errors creeping into the inner workings of my trading mind. Am I maintaining my discipline? Am I adding to winners? Am I impulsive?

You may look at the chart and think I did okay. I look at the chart and I wonder why I got out. The pain of having missed out on the rally towards the end of the day was greater than the pleasure from making back what I had lost earlier in the day.

PRESSING WINNERS

Adding to winners is habitual for me. I have new and experienced traders following me on YouTube and Telegram exclaiming they want to know how I do it.

One simple way of doing it is to look over the prior trading days, and come up with a number of points at which you will want to add to your position. For example, you may look at Euro Dollar and conclude you want to add to your position at every 10-pip interval.

I went about my approach in a different manner. I think it is best illustrated through the use of a theoretical explanation.

I want to trade the FTSE 100 Index, and I am looking for an approach to adding to my winning trades. How do I go about doing that?

Figure 19

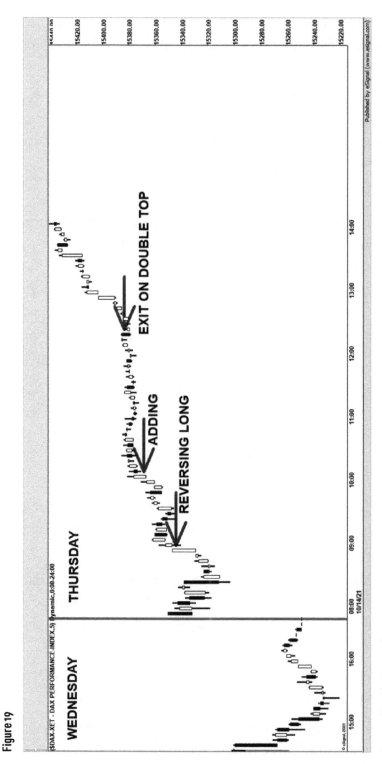

Source: eSignal (esignal.com)

STEP 1

I need to establish what the historical volatility is in this index. I use a measure called Average True Range (ATR). When using it I carefully differentiate between periods in which I don't want to trade the product, and those in which I do want to trade the product.

For example, the volatility of the FTSE Index on a five-minute chart during the night could be around 4 points, while the volatility on a five-minute chart at the open at 8 am GMT is around 14 points. That is a significant difference.

Say for the sake of argument that I have established that the volatility is equal to 10 pips/10 points where I day trade the FTSE Index on the time frame I prefer to trade.

We call that value N.

N = 10

My stop-loss is 2 × N.

STEP 2

Establish how much money you want to risk on a trade. This is a percentage function of your account value. Say you have £10,000 in your trading account, and you decide you want to risk 2% of the account.

Hence 2% of £10,000 = £200.

STEP 3

Now I establish my trading size *unit*, which is essentially how big my trading size is.

If N = 10

Risk = 2N

Monetary Risk = £200

Then my trading size unit will be £200 / 20 = £10

STEP 4

I can then argue that I want to *add* to my position at every ½N. I think this is where your own research should come into play. However, for the sake of the argument, I will take you through an example, based on the numbers above.

EXAMPLE

I buy the FTSE Index at 7,500.

My stop is 20 points.

My risk is £10 per point.

My *add-on* is at every ½N. This means I add at every 5-point increment.

The FTSE Index now trades at 7,505. I buy one more unit, meaning I am now buying £10 a point at 7,505.

I now have two open positions:

    Long 7,500 with stop-loss at 7,480.

    Long at 7,505 with stop-loss at 7,485.

As you can quickly gather, this will cause a bigger loss than anticipated if I do not move my stop-loss up on the first position.

Before I enter the second position, I have already planned to move my stop-loss up by ½N. I will move the stop-loss up on the first position by 5 points. This means that the stop-losses on the first and second positions are identical. My total risk is now 35 points.

As I hope you can see, this way of trading can quickly materialise a larger loss than perhaps you had wanted it to. It is for this reason I urge you to consider variations of this method, such as adding with smaller stake size on the second, third and fourth positions.

You may ask, "Why add at all?"

Because by adding, I am actively combatting the brain's proclivity to scaling down risk. Our brains want to take profit. I am doing the opposite. I am adding to my position.

REAL-LIFE EXAMPLE

The following chart shows the Dow Jones Index on a *trend day*. I define a *trend day* as a day when the market opens at the high or the low of the day, and closes at the low or the high of the day.

The problem with trend days is that you won't know it was a trend day until the day is over. So, you have to make an assumption, based around what you see on the chart, about whether you think it is a trend day.

I have researched the price action behaviour of the Dow Jones Index over 18 years. I have identified a handful of *first hour* patterns, which I believe are precursors for trend days. One of those patterns is a *gap down* after a *gap up* day, where the gap down is not filled within the first hour.

Figure 20 shows a positive Thursday. The trade I want to show you took place on the Friday. Friday is notorious for producing lasting trends, often leading to trend days, especially on Fridays at the beginning or end of the month.

I have also included a screenshot of my trading monitor.

Figure 20

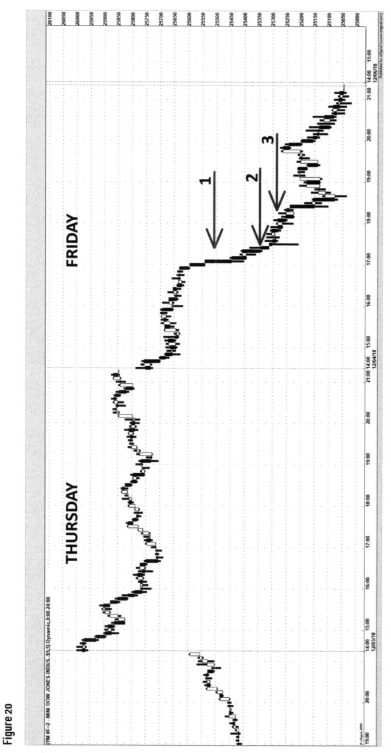

Source: eSignal (esignal.com)

Wall Street	3,000.0	25419.6	25135.9	kr851,150.00
	500.0	25458	25135.9	kr161,500.00
	700.0	25455	25135.9	kr224,000.00
	350.0	25469	25135.9	kr116,725.00
	450.0	25455	25135.9	kr143,775.00
	200.0	25441	25135.9	kr61,100.00
	300.0	25329	25135.9	kr58,050.00
	250.0	25356	25135.9	kr55,250.00
	125.0	25258	25135.9	kr15,312.50
	125.0	25259	25135.9	kr15,437.50

The top line shows my overall exposure. It states I am short 3,000 in Wall Street. My average entry is 25,419.6. The current price is 25,135.9. The 3,000 means I am short 3,000 Danish kroner per point, which equates to about 500 US dollars per point movement in the Dow.

So, for every point the Dow Index drops, I make 3000 kroner, and vice versa. For every point it rallies, I lose 3000 kroner. At the time of the screen shot I am in profit by 851,000 kroner.

Below my total exposure, you see each of the entries, which add up to 3,000.

If you look at the previous chart, you will see the numbers 1, 2, and 3. Those are points where I am adding to my position.

At Point 1 on the chart, I start selling short. I scale into my short position over five entries. Those are the first five entries you see below my total exposure.

At Point 2, I add more short positions. I do so because the market is weak, and I am certain a trend day is developing. I add about 25% more to my short position at Point 2. At Point 3, I add about 10% more to my short position

As the market moves lower, I add to my positions, as I have been trained to do. I move my stop-loss down as well. What you are unable to see on the chart is that initially the market moved against me.

What I am doing here is critical to your understanding of fear. I have been under water on my position, and now I am finally making money. My brain has had to endure pain during the loss period, and I am now being sent signals from my mind to relieve my brain of the pain it felt during the losing period (15 minutes earlier).

I counteract this pain by actively doing the very thing that causes me pain. I am embracing the discomfort by compounding it. This is required if I am to actively engage in behaviour that is the opposite of the 90%'s. You will notice that my add-on is not a big position. Yet, it serves to reinforce the right kind of behaviour.

The Dow falls strongly. I am in the safe zone now. My core position cannot be threatened. My stops are placed at breakeven. However, I am still prepared to let this trade turn into an insignificant trade (small profit trade) in the *hope* that it will turn into a significant trade.

You must find your own level of risk temperance. Once I was asked "If you keep adding to your trades, when do you take profits?" That is a great question. I use the charts to take profits. If I double bottom on a chart, and I am short, then I might be tempted to take profit.

Alternatively – and this is a really good trick – I will place my stop-loss where I would want to get into the market, but in the other direction. For example, in this case, if I am short the Dow Jones Index I might place my stop-loss at the price level where I would turn into a buyer of the index.

Although I am 100 points in profit, I am by no means relaxing. I am adding to my position again and again, in smaller increments, in order to reinforce the right behaviour.

The trade had the potential to turn into a spectacular trade. It didn't. The Dow bounced strongly (before falling again), and although I made a profit, it was not the amount you see on the screenshot.

That is very important for me to get across to you, because I think it is important that you establish some criteria for how much of your *paper profits* you are prepared to give away in order to capture the really big days.

There are days when I come to work, and I just want to capture 20–30 points, and then be done. Not every day has hundreds of points available in it.

Then there are days when the market starts out very strongly or very weakly, and you think to yourself, "This could be a really big day."

I have a philosophy to trading that means I am prepared to sacrifice profits in order to discover how big the profit can get. If you don't have that philosophy, you will never discover how big the profit can get.

If you always think of potential targets, using technical analysis, you are most likely just talking your way out of a good trade. You might be using technical measures to time your exit, but I don't subscribe to this method. There is a reason for that. When the market is trending, and I am on board the trend with a position, I hope that the market will close that night at its strongest/weakest for the day.

It happens on at least 20% of all trading days in stock indices. Yes, I have had plenty of disappointments, but I have had sufficient stellar days to make it part of my philosophy.

DAX INDEX – TRADING EXAMPLE

Let me show you another example of a trade where I added to my positions. However, this time I will show you what I saw at the time of the trade. See Figure 21.

I am not on board the first push down. I look at the rebound for an opportunity to short the DAX Index. On the next image you can see my initial position entries highlighted in box 1.

Figure 21

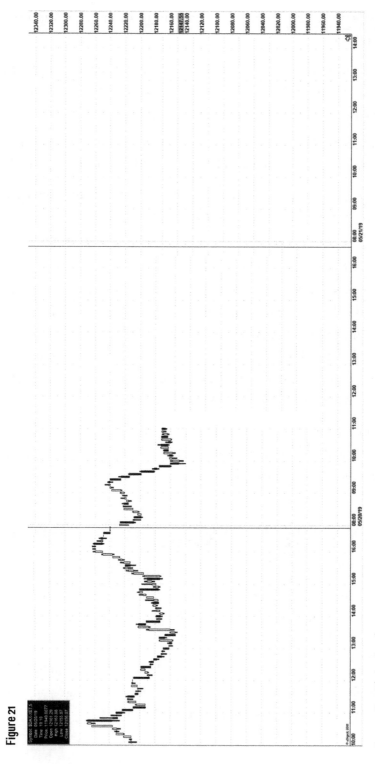

Source: eSignal (esignal.com)

Product/Trade	Quantity				Open P/L
Germany 30	5,000.0	12130.7	12050.5		kr401,080.00
	500.0	12164.7	12050.5		kr57,100.00
	500.0	12165.2	12050.5		kr57,350.00
1	200.0	12166.8	12050.5		kr23,260.00
	100.0	12167.5	12050.5		kr11,700.00
	100.0	12162.3	12050.5		kr11,180.00
	100.0	12163.7	12050.5		kr11,320.00
	100.0	12156.3	12050.5		kr10,580.00
	100.0	12156.0	12050.5		kr10,550.00
	100.0	12155.8	12050.5		kr10,530.00
2	200.0	12146.3	12050.5		kr19,160.00
	1,000.0	12110.8	12050.5		kr60,300.00
	1,000.0	12110.8	12050.5		kr60,300.00
	500.0	12108.0	12050.5		kr28,750.00
	500.0	12108.5	12050.5		kr29,000.00

DAX finally caves in and resumes its downtrend, as shown in Figure 22. You can see my subsequent short entries in box 2. There are a couple of things I would like you to see here:

1. I am not afraid to sell short something that has already fallen in price. This is consistent with what the majority of people do not want to do.

2. I scale into the position in this example, and I add aggressively to my short position once my position is in profit.

I urge you to contemplate how you can introduce the element of *adding to winners* into your trading. I am not interested in rewriting your trading plan. I am not interested in turning you into a copy of me. I am interested in trying to make you understand the value of *pain* in trading, as a barometer for adding to positions.

If it is uncomfortable, then it is probably the right thing to do.

Figure 22

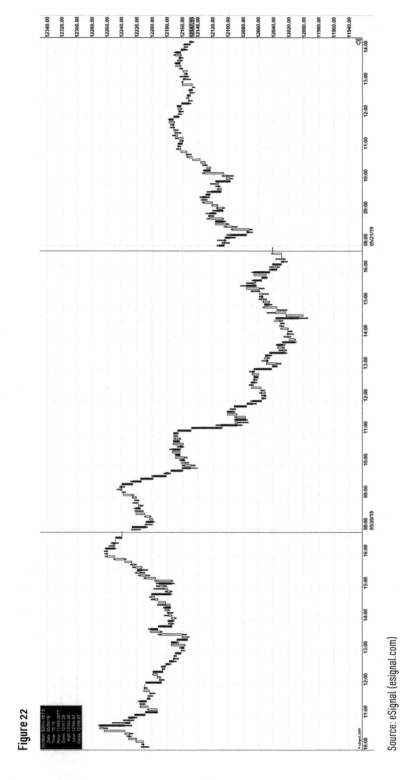

Source: eSignal (esignal.com)

I will repeat something I mentioned earlier. I think you should give serious contemplation to the question of why people in general find it easier to add to a losing trade than a winning trade.

I don't ever want to be accused of glorifying trading. It is a risky proposition. Twenty years ago most brokers in Europe didn't have what we today know as negative balance protection. Today, it is a legal requirement. It means that you can't lose more money than is available on your trading account.

You can still lose a lot more than you anticipate, especially if you add to positions, like I do.

As you become better at trading, you will want to trade bigger and bigger size, and the market on a big position doesn't have to change direction by a lot before you give away a big portion of your open profits.

If you want proof of that, here it is. This was a perfectly good-looking DAX position which turned from being very profitable to showing a significant loss. It starts well with a short position at 11,288. I then add to the position as the DAX Index falls. Then the market reverses, and I add a little more at the old top.

At the point of the screenshot I am short 4,500 kroner per point, and I am losing 25 points. I close the position shortly after for a loss.

4,500.0	11289.4	11314.0	kr−110,5100.00
300.0	11288.3	11314.0	kr−7,710.00
350.0	11286.8	11314.0	kr−9,520.00
400.0	11285.2	11314.0	kr−11,520.00
500.0	11285.0	11314.0	kr−14,500.00
500.0	11279.0	11314.0	kr−17,500.00
500.0	11274.8	11314.0	kr−19,600.00
450.0	11295.2	11314.0	kr−8,460.00
500.0	11293.2	11314.0	kr−10,400.00
500.0	11292.7	11314.0	kr−10,650.00
500.0	11312.7	11314.0	kr650.00

UNCOMFORTABLE

There are no shortcuts in the trading industry, any more than there are shortcuts in, say, professional sports. I expect to get uncomfortable during the trading. At times it feels like the minutes last for hours. My impatience to do something is raging within me. I am battling my own emotions more than I am battling the markets.

Finally, when I am in a position, my mind has something to occupy itself with. Be careful what you ask for! Maybe the position is showing a loss, so now I am battling my subconscious mind, which wants the position to run a little longer.

My conscious mind has a stop-loss, but my subconscious mind wants to me to remove it. It doesn't want to lose.

It could be the position is going well. Now my subconscious wants me to take my profits. It loves the gratification of a good profit. So, I am battling it whether I am winning or losing on my trades.

The key to victory starts with being mindful of the existence of *two brains*. The ability to anticipate your enemy's next move is crucial. The subconscious brain is a rather simple beast. It just wants to avoid pain.

For the subconscious brain there are two pains in trading. There is the pain of seeing a profit. When it sees a profit, it wants you to close it because then it doesn't have to deal with the pain of seeing the profit disappear. Then there is the pain of loss. When the subconscious brain sees a loss, it wants you to hold on to the position a little longer and a little longer. Otherwise, it will have to deal with taking the loss. As long as the position is open, there is always hope.

In a nutshell, what separates the 10% of winners from the 90% of losers is which brain they are listening to. It took me many years to realise this. I developed a system for my mind, a training program that enabled me to withstand the influences of the emotional subconscious brain on my trading decisions.

During the Round the Clock Trader event referred to previously, a guest asked me if I wasn't afraid that the market would turn back up the moment I went short.

Who do you think was really asking that question? It was the part of his mind controlled by fear. Of course, the market might very well turn around. I would lie if I said that had never happened. It probably happens five times out of ten. So, the real question to be asked is this:

what would cause you more pain?

1. You sell short and the market reverses back up.
2. You do nothing and the market reverses back up.
3. You sell short and the market continues lower.
4. You do nothing and the market continues lower.

OPTION 1

I sell short and the darn market moves against me again. It is annoying, but the stop-loss will take care of my exit. At least I can say that I followed my plan.

OPTION 2

I do nothing and the market moves back up. I might be happy, but I have just trained my mind not to follow the plan, and I was rewarded for it.

I was rewarded by not selling short, which would have lost me money, and my mind is now congratulating me for my excellent chart reading skills, but for all the wrong reasons.

OPTION 3

I sell short, like I am supposed to, and the market follows through to the downside. Instead of clapping my small paws in joy, I am proactive, and I add to my winning trade. I am doing absolutely everything I am meant to do.

OPTION 4

I decide not to follow the plan of shorting, and the market moves aggressively lower. I would have made all the lost money back from the first trade, but I do not.

I can't speak for you, but I will tell you how I feel about it. It causes me more emotional pain to miss a move because I didn't follow through on my plan than when I followed through with my plan.

WHAT IS TOO FAR?

Another question that came in after the short trade was this: "Were you not concerned that the market had already moved *too far*? Do you not think you had already missed the boat?"

The person who asked this question is most likely the same person who would not buy the DAX because it had already rallied 1% on the day.

This is the supermarket analogy all over. We seek out bargains, but we avoid buying items that have risen in price.

It is a mental illusion. You can't say the DAX is too expensive just because it has rallied 1% on the day. We do not want to buy something that is already going up. We would rather wait until it comes down again to buy it, because then it is *cheaper*.

Similarly, we do not want to sell short something that is already going down. We want to wait for it to rise again and sell it when it is higher (more *expensive*) because it gives us better value.

In principle, I don't disagree with these statements, but here is the flaw: that is what everyone else wants to do, and the majority tend to be wrong. Correction: they don't tend to be wrong; they *are* wrong. Sure, they are right 60% of the time, but when they are wrong they are *really* wrong. How do you know where the top or the bottom is? I have seen a lot of trading systems, but none of them had an acceptable success ratio of predicting tops or bottoms.

This is why I say that you should *buy* strength and you should *sell* weakness. Buy high, sell higher; sell low, buy back lower. Will I miss the absolute turning points? Yes, I will. Top pickers and bottom pickers soon become cotton pickers.

When I am distressed about profits disappearing, I remind myself of the story of a US super trader whose reputation for doing the right thing under pressure is legendary. His name is Paul Tudor Jones.

He was once watching the market and, as it had been rising all morning, he had been buying steadily. He was long several hundred contracts showing a good profit.

Suddenly the market jolted lower for no apparent reason. Without blinking, he sold out all his long positions, and as the market continued to fall, he started to sell short the market too. One of his colleagues who didn't know he had commenced shorting the market commented on the fall and said this was a good chance to start buying.

The conversation, edited for expletives, went on as follows:

"Are you mad?" said Paul.

"What do you mean?" said the colleague.

"You must be mad. The market has just broken 100 points in 15 minutes, and you are looking to *buy* it?"

"Well, what would you do?"

"Let's put it this way, I am certainly not looking to *buy* it here."

"Well, would you sell them short here?"

"Of course I would!"

"But they have come down so far."

"Exactly, that's the point."

"Right," said the colleague. "Well just how far would the market have to fall before you started to buy it?"

"As long as it is going down, why would I buy it?"

"Because it's so cheap, it's an absolute bargain. It's 100 points cheaper than it was 15 minutes ago."

"Forget cheap. Forget expensive. It's just numbers on a page."

"But I don't understand. If it kept going down, where would you try and buy it?"

"If it kept going down, I'd want to be selling it, not buying it. If it kept going down, I would sell it down to zero."

"And if it was going up?"

If it kept going up, I'd buy it to infinity."

I absolutely love this story. Having seen Paul Tudor Jones trade, you sense his energy, his intensity and determination, and his utter conviction in whatever he does. He doesn't just say, "Sell short." He shouts, "*Sell short!*" stamps his feet and swings his hands.

I admire his mental agility – flowing from being convinced on the long side to turning the position to the short side. Sadly, this is one trait that is hard to acquire. I know some traders with decades of trading experience who are unable to *flip the switch* and go from being long to being short.

FINDING A LOW

Trying to find the low in a stock can be a costly affair. We all make mistakes, but how costly is the mistake going to be? I remember very vividly watching a CNBC show called *Mad Money*, during the financial crisis in 2008.

On the show Jim Cramer received an email from a viewer asking about the health of Bear Stearns. Now I am sure that if Mr Cramer had an opportunity to go back in time he would most certainly amend what he said in that broadcast.

He basically shouted at the screen, saying that Bear Stearns was fine. But a few days later Bear Stearns was gone, done and dusted, never to be seen again.

You may recall my first brush with meeting clients back in 2001. I gave them the not-so-welcome advice to get the hell out of their Marconi shares. Would you believe it if I told you that history repeated itself in 2007?

It is easy to be swayed by a *supermarket mentality* when we are trading. As I mentioned previously in the book, when we go into a supermarket, we are drawn towards the special offers. When I look at my shopping basket from this weekend, I see things that I wouldn't normally buy.

Of course, I would need these things at some point or another. We all need toilet paper. We all need dishwasher tablets, and we all need hand soap. The reason why they were in my shopping basket this week was because they were on offer. Who can resist a 50% discount?

But a 50% discount in a supermarket is not the same thing as a 50% discount in the financial markets. Many clients of City Index, the broker I worked at for more than eight years, came face to face with this reality during the financial crisis from 2007 to 2009.

In 2006, after having done very little for years, a stock called Northern Rock went on a tear. It rallied 50% in months. There was no real interest from City Index clients in the stock during the rally phase.

However, when it began to slide back down again afterwards, the interest rose. It was as if Northern Rock had the same effect on investors that half-price toilet paper has on shoppers in a supermarket.

Northern Rock became quite a lively traded stock. The more Northern Rock fell in price, the more people got interested in the stock. At one point I received a phone call on a Saturday morning at home. At this point Northern Rock had slipped from 1200 pence down to around 500 pence.

The person on the other end of the phone was a stranger to me. He had picked up my business card at one of the talks I had given on technical analysis. He apologised for calling me so early on a Saturday morning, but he and his friend had decided to invest in Northern Rock. They had decided to get the opinion of a professional, just to double check whether it was a good idea.

Apart from being rather annoyed at being woken up at 7 am on a Saturday by a stranger, I was also annoyed with the question. At this point Northern Rock was in freefall. I roughly said the following to the stranger:

> Look, I don't know what is going on with Northern Rock, but there is something horribly wrong. Although the general market is declining too, Northern Rock is declining much more.

> What I am afraid of is that there is something amiss that we don't know about, and it has yet to be known to the market. It feels as if someone somewhere knows something is horribly wrong, and they are selling out while they can.

I told him that I had many clients who had said exactly what he was saying now, but about Marconi five years earlier. Fortunes were lost by clients who kept buying Marconi, even though it was falling and falling, because they engaged in bargain hunting. It had been horrible to see the losses our most valuable clients endured simply because they did not want to admit they were on the wrong side of a bad share.

I said to him: "From a trader's perspective, you are engaging in a very dangerous activity. If you buy Northern Rock now, it will be very difficult for you to have a meaningful stop-loss. You are essentially trying to catch the falling knife. You talk as if Northern Rock is the only bank in the world worth investing in.

"You talk about Northern Rock as if it couldn't go bust. You talk about it as if the fact that it is 200 years old means that things couldn't get worse before they get better. You even said it yourself: Northern Rock is too big to fail. It means you are already to some extent aware of the danger here." I asked him if he remembered Barings Bank. He did.

"There is a second reason why I don't think it's a good idea you buy Northern Rock," I continued. "Let's say you are fortunate enough to witness a turnaround in the fortunes of Northern Rock. You will have trained your mind to think that it is perfectly okay to buy into things that are falling. This works perfectly in a supermarket. Toilet paper has a practical use. Soap has a practical use, so when you are provided with an opportunity to purchase these items at a 50% discount, you should do it.

"However, to believe that the financial markets offer discounts akin to what you're seeing in a supermarket is ludicrous. The financial markets are not a supermarket with special offers."

Eventually Northern Rock went bust. The British government had to guarantee customers' savings. That didn't stop panic scenes as people queued up to get their money out.

THINKING RIGHT

As you read this anecdote, you might think it could never happen to you. Perhaps you are right. I am not going to suggest otherwise, but I would like to ask you a simple question.

Imagine you have two investments, Investment A and Investment B. Each investment had equal starting value of $100,000.

Investment A is doing well. It is up 50%.

Investment B on the other hand is not performing. It is down 50%.

You are now in a situation where you need $50,000. What do you do?

1. Close a third of Investment A to raise $50,000?

2. Close investment B to raise $50,000?

When I asked this question to a group of investors at a conference in Copenhagen recently, the overwhelming majority opted for option 1. They would close enough of investment A to raise the $50,000.

Why do you think that is? Why do you think people close the investment that is doing well?

My theory is it all boils doing to how people react to taking a loss. Are they able to take a loss and move on? Or are they so averse to taking a loss because as long as the position is open, there is hope it will come good again?

Of course, it is impossible to say exactly how you would react in this situation, but I don't have to rely on fictitious examples to get an answer. If you recall the chapter where I spoke about the 43 million trades executed by 25,000 traders, you will remember that those traders lost more on their losing trades than they won on their winning trades.

Emotionally, a loss is clearly felt much harder than a win. Otherwise, there would be no reason for this anomaly. Human beings postpone making decisions that will cause pain. It is the reason why we let losing trades run.

We want the instant gratification, but we want to delay the pain. Hope dies last. As long as the losing position is open, there is hope.

THE JUNKIE AND THE CEO

I use an analogy to illustrate the concept I have just explained: it is akin to firing the CEO of a successful Fortune 500 company and betting your money on the junkie turning his life around.

Crude? Yes. The junkie might turn his life around, but I think the odds of the CEO continuing his successful run are higher than those of the junkie turning a corner for the better.

That is why I am arguing that trading is so much more than technical analysis. That is why I am arguing that we need to learn to handle losses a lot better than the general population does, because they handle them *very* poorly, and as a result they are generally unable to make money from speculation.

CONTROL YOUR MIND – CONTROL YOUR FUTURE

I am not a masochist. Nothing could be further from the truth. If I do tend to dwell on pain, it is more a reflection of pain's role in the context of trading profitably. What I'm attempting to do is a difficult endeavour. I'm trying to explain why 90% of all people fail in achieving their hopes and dreams when it comes to trading.

When so many people commit the same mistakes over and over, there must be a deeper meaning that has yet to be uncovered. Naturally I'm hoping that by now you will have a much greater understanding of what it is that is going wrong.

My own motto is: *control your mind – control your future*. Doing so requires constant vigilance. You have to own your life. If you don't own it, you are not the boss. You have to take full responsibility for everything that you do.

You must be the master of your own kingdom. You can't walk through life with your eyes half shut. You have to walk through life with your eyes fully open. You have to know what you are getting into – be prepared. You have to take possession of your life.

This is a thought process you have to constantly *reaffirm*. Our minds tend to drift. There are so many distractions in life, so much superficial noise that doesn't bring substance but that our brains are attracted to nonetheless. The brain would rather look at Facebook and YouTube than sit in quiet contemplation.

The *drifter brain* needs to be controlled through daily vigilance, whether it be through a mantra or meditation or whatever you decide suits you best. As a famous doctor once said when asked what exercise is best for us humans: "It's the one you do". It doesn't matter whether you meditate or write a diary or do whatever other practice you choose to centre yourself, *so long as you do it*.

There needs to be a regular time in your day where you remind yourself of your purpose, of who you are. The world is full of temptations that distort a healthy self image. The temptations take us away from who we are by telling us that who we are is not enough.

But you are enough.

Being a good trader really has little to do with tools and charts. It has a lot to do with fighting our humanness. If you really want to trade the markets using leverage, engaging in high-octane speculation, you have to learn to desensitise your normal emotional response mechanism to fear, greed and other delightful human reactions. You have to fight your humanness.

DISGUST

MANY YEARS AGO, when I was just a young man, I had a girlfriend. She was my first real girlfriend, and I was her first real boyfriend. We were young, and we were very much in love.

My girlfriend was a little round bodily, which I found very attractive. She, however, did not like her body image, so she began to diet. She had dieted before, but had always failed to sustain a weight loss plan. Now she was in love, and her motivation shifted into another gear. The weight loss became quite dramatic, and it led me and her family down a path that pains me to write about.

Anorexia is a serious psychiatric disorder, but (and forgive me for using a tragic story to illustrate a point about behavioural change) it is an interesting motivational phenomenon.

We are hardwired to eat. We need no training to eat. Yet somehow this hardwired pattern is overridden by a social motivation: the desire not to be overweight. This force, this motivation, is so strong in patients with an eating disorder that it proves to be impervious to both medical and psychological treatment.

What is the basis for this powerful motivation? It isn't chanting, and it isn't positive self-talk. As I understand it, my girlfriend was motivated by love, but more importantly by disgust. She was disgusted by anything that looked and felt fat and overweight. This force was so strong it could disrupt her hardwired pattern of eating food.

As humans we are driven forward by forces. Those forces can be born out of a desire to move away from something, or they can be born out of a desire to move towards something. I happen to be a person who is primarily motivated to *move away* from something.

I grew up in a wealthy part of Denmark, and I attended a school for the well-to-do. Then my parents divorced, and I went from living in a big house with an enormous garden to living in a one-bedroom flat, where my father would sleep on a pull-out sofa bed in the living room.

I was a young boy at a time when all my school friends wore Levi's denims and Lacoste shirts. There was no money for that in my life, and it created a sense of inferiority in me.

As soon as I was old enough, I started taking afterschool jobs in order to earn money. What did I spend it on? You guessed it. Brand clothes.

I also became a prolific hoarder of money, a saver, if you like. I took great pride in depositing my wage cheques in the bank and seeing my account balance grow. I moved away from poverty.

In my belief system and in my experience, *away-oriented* goal setting is a much stronger motivational force than *towards-oriented*, but I accept that this is an individual preference. You can test for yourself where your preference lies, using a simplistic scenario. What would compel you to lose weight more: a picture of you in perfect shape or a picture of you where you are obese?

I asked my circle of friends what they would prefer, and all agreed that they would find the obese picture a stronger motivator than the perfect picture, although a few did comment that they would probably still like to have both. Fair point.

I believe that disgust is a much stronger emotion than joy or happiness. We all have reasons to be happy every day, but we tend to forget that. However, disgust is not something we are likely to forget.

You won't forget the rotten milk you drank by mistake, nor will you forget the client of yours who had such repugnant breath that you nearly threw up.

Ed Seykota once said that everybody gets what they want from the markets. When I read that, I dismissed it. I wanted to win, but I wasn't winning, so I clearly wasn't getting what I wanted. End of story.

It annoyed me that he had said that. The thought of never being able to trade profitably consumed me. I had spent so much time studying, researching, testing, formulating plans, calculating ratios that I really didn't know what more I could do.

If you look around in your life, you are likely to be able to find examples of dramatic changes induced by disgust. What gets a person to finally commit to a goal is reaching the point of disgust. I got disgusted with my trading over a long period of time. The pattern was always the same:

1. Trade like a wizard.

2. Become over-confident.

3. Blow up the account.

I became so sick of it. Positive intentions, sticky notes with mantras on my trading monitor, and self-help exercises don't possess nearly the motivational force of physical disgust with oneself.

If disgust can turn eating into a behaviour to be avoided, and if disgust can turn an alcoholic's drinking into a thing of the past, then disgust can also turn you into the trader you would be proud of looking at in the mirror.

I am sorry if I have shocked you. Those of you who know me well will probably be taken back by my extreme steps to ensure my pattern of behaviour in the trading arena is exemplary.

I am not going back to the rollercoaster ride I was on in my early trading days. I was so disgusted with the amount of money I lost. It was embarrassing.

We are most apt to change a pattern once we become truly disgusted by it. Would you continue to do business with someone who violated your trust and stole money from you? No, you'd become so disgusted with such a dishonest character that you would cut all ties with them.

Well, that person is you when your own patterns violate your contract with yourself and cause you to lose money consistently. Once you become truly disgusted with your own patterns, you'll shun them altogether.

A trader is losing and continues to lose because he doesn't want to change. Change is hard work. I began plotting my trades on the chart when the day was over. I put a marker where my entry was and where my exit was. It was horrible. It was like incriminating yourself over and over. I was disgusted with my recklessness.

I had to face up to the fact that I was actually an awful trader. I was like the guy who could recite the entire technical analysis syllabus for the Master Technician exam, but I could not stop myself from

1. Overtrading out of boredom.

2. Overtrading out of anger and a desire to get revenge.

3. Impatient trading – jumping the gun.

4. Trading against the trend – trying to catch the low of the day.

5. Fearful trading – by cutting my winners short out of fear the profit would disappear.

6. Constantly averaging in lower and lower – i.e., adding to losing trades.

ALCOHOL

When you are a successful trader, you make good money. My friend and trader mentor Larry Pesavento instilled in me the passion for *passing on.* Larry himself is an inspiring trader, but his passion for helping others is equally admirable.

One project I support is to help people dealing with alcohol issues. I do so by offering anyone who sincerely desires to quit drinking a book that helped me truly understand the nature of the addiction trap.

I developed a drinking problem in the aftermath of a painful breakup. I drank to forget. I was in love. I was a fool. She left me. I started drinking.

The problem was that I didn't seem to be able to stop myself from drinking. This carried on for many months. I could not stop myself from drinking, so I sought out help. I remember vividly standing up at an Alcoholics Anonymous (AA) meeting saying, "My name is Tom Hougaard. I am an alcoholic."

It was horrible, but at the same time it was relieving. I felt like a fraud. I felt there was inconsistency in my life. I was outwardly a success. I had two cars. One was a luxury SUV, the other an Audi R8. I lived in a nice part of town, overlooking the sea. What did I have to be unhappy about? Well, for one, I had no control over myself and my drinking.

Standing at an AA meeting is like being stripped naked for the whole world to see. They see your fat ass, your tiny willy, your saggy boobs, your cellulite, your scars, your spots, your pimples, your swellings, your bald head and whatever bodily imperfections you can imagine. It is absolutely everything you don't want, and you have a hall full of eyes watching you.

But by the end of the exercise you realise the truth. You break yourself down so that you can survive, so that you can be reborn as the person that you really want to be. A fresh start. Vanity thrown on the rubbish pile. Clean canvas. Here I am. This is me.

The walls are ready to be decorated however you want. Exactly the same model is used to train elite soldiers. They are pushed beyond their breaking point. Then they are put back together again, stronger, wiser and with an unshakable faith in their own strength, their own abilities and their determination to get a job done – no matter what.

No one in their right mind enjoys exposing themselves like this. It is why we get defensive. It is why we fight our corner. Our identity is being questioned. Call it ego, call it identity, call it what you want, but no one likes having their intelligence questioned. It is a lot less painful to continue down the known path than to stop, evaluate, and turn around.

There is only a slight, nagging pain when you choose to continue down the known path, and you can soothe your inner pain by reminding yourself that you are not alone. There is power in numbers, even when everyone is wrong. But you soon find yourself being disgusted by your own lack of progress, your own inability to stop the behaviour that is troubling you.

Attending AA meetings was rock bottom for me. I evaluated. I got honest with myself. The pain was relentless because everything was new, and I felt naked, very alone and exposed.

And yet, that is power! There is power in being honest. There is power in standing up and saying to the world and yourself: "This is who I am, and I don't like it! In fact I hate it. I am embarrassed by it, but it is what it is. It is a clean slate. It is a fresh start. It is like a forest fire. It clears the debris. New growth can start."

I have not touched alcohol for six years and I know I never will. It wasn't the AA that finally helped me; it was healthy living advocate Jason Vale. I have never met the man, but I want to thank him for setting my life on a good path. I am certain that no one has bought more copies of his book about alcohol dependency than I have. I send them to people all over the world.

Jason describes better than anyone the trap of alcohol. Reading his book helped me understand the nature of addiction on an entirely different level, and I found it easy to stop drinking from day one!

You may ask what this has to do with trading. Rightly so. The answer is simple: if you have some trading experience, and it is not turning out to be how you want it to be, you have a choice. You can carry on, thinking that things will change. I can tell you they won't, but you will probably not listen to me.

Or you can take my advice. You did after all make it all the way to this section of the book, so maybe there is room for improvement. You can strip yourself naked (metaphorically speaking), and get honest with yourself. You can stop trading, and start reviewing. You can begin to understand what it is you are consistently doing that causes you not to make money trading.

Take yourself apart, clean up the process, take on board my guidance for the mental side of trading, put yourself back together again, fund a small account and start with an entirely fresh mindset and approach.

THE DRIFTER MIND

How our minds work is fascinating. The brain can be our best friend or our worst enemy. When I give talks in public, my own life mantra is written on virtually every PowerPoint page of any presentation I give.

Control your mind – control your future.

You have to want to do what you do. You can live a life that is authentic to your soul, or you can live the life you think people want you to live.

You can be authentic and own your life and take responsibility for everything you do. If you don't take ownership of your life, you are not the boss. You have to take full responsibility for everything that you do.

Why would you live life any other way?

Why be subservient? You must be the master of your own kingdom. But brace yourself. You will be forced to make many difficult decisions, and you cannot count on your mind to back you up if your determination wanders a little.

You can't just walk through your life with your eyes half open. You have to know where you are going. You have to take possession of your life. It would be nice if you could rely on your friends and family, but when it comes to your life's journey, you are on your own. It is your responsibility.

Part of that journey, including your trading journey, is to discover your weaknesses. You have to know where your mind lets you down. For the vast majority of people in the world, this will include their mind's tendency to wander.

You see, all of us know what to do. All of us have the knowledge to do what needs to be done, but the path from knowledge to action, where we implement our knowledge, is elusive for many people in many areas of their lives.

Your mind will drift. This is unfortunate but perfectly natural. The solution is trivial, and it is powerful. You have to constantly reaffirm your purpose. Whether you meditate or talk to yourself while you brush your teeth in the morning, there needs to be some period in your day when you remember your purpose. There must be a time to remind yourself where you want to go, what you want to do.

One thing I can't always rely on is my ability to act in my own best self-interest. My mind needs constant guidance and direction. I don't know why that is, but it is. I suspect the majority of the population of the planet is put together like I am. They just haven't realised it yet, so they drift through life, rather than taking charge. This doesn't mean they can't be financially successful, but wouldn't it be nice to be both financially and spiritually fulfilled? Your job after all is that thing that you do the most, outside of sleeping.

I am a professional trader. I cannot afford to go into the trading ring without being 100% mentally prepared. My profession is a mind game like nothing else. If I want to win, I have to focus on what is important now. So Ed Seykota was right, much to my chagrin. I did get what I deserved, because I was only good at one part of the game. I was good at the technical part.

I don't like this metaphor, but being good at the technical part of trading is like being good at putting together a sniper rifle; what good does that do you when you go into combat and you don't know how to handle yourself?

I actively take control of my inner world. I have to give myself enough confidence to reassure myself that I have enough to go out and kick ass in the markets every day.

To make that challenge even more real, I post my trades for the world to see. I have never consciously thought about why I do that, until someone recently asked me. I realised that I do it because it keeps me accountable. It keeps me focused.

I have been as lost as they come. I tell you that not to inspire *you* to get lost, nor to evoke sympathy, nor to tell a tale of rags-to-riches, but to make sure you understand that exposing your weaknesses will be a good thing.

Your mind is a tool. If you let it delude you into thinking all is well, you will not get the success you want in trading or in life.

Losing and failing might be a knock to the ego, but it is rocket fuel for growth. It sounds like I am trying to write a self-help manual for procrastination, a bestselling inspirational book. But I am describing honesty. When you are honest with yourself, in the company of yourself, or on a podium in front of 40 alcoholics, or whatever the setting may be, you just took a step that 99% of the population don't ever contemplate taking. You already started the journey to winning.

So, the journey starts with technical knowledge acquisition and continues indefinitely with the constant evolution of both the technical and mental training.

Technical training is part of my day-to-day job, but the mental part needs more dedicated focus, otherwise it gets lost in the noise of the outside world. I need dedicated time to give that brain of mine a workout.

I want to show you one of the mental warmup images that I go through before the trading day starts. It gives me the visual evidence I need to act in a manner that is aligned with what I am trying to achieve.

This example happened a while ago, but it could happen any day of the week if I don't mentally prepare myself. Figure 23 tells the tale in all its glory.

I short a double top off the open. I am so certain that my research is right. The market will fall.

I don't have a problem with the first short position. I have a problem with the four subsequent ones. I could even forgive myself for the last one, because at least I am shorting weakness. This is unstructured and undisciplined trading. I don't care how certain I am of something happening. If it isn't happening, don't pursue it as if it is. Showing you is so embarrassing!

This is part of my preparation. It has been the most useful tool to build mental stamina and discipline. It reminds me of everything that is weak in me. It reminds me of how my mind, if left unchecked and untrained, will go on a rampage to seek excitement and gratification.

One of the best ways to increase profits is to use goalsetting and visualisations to align the conscious and subconscious with making profits. I use fear to achieve my goals. I imagine trading a size which even in my mind makes me uncomfortable.

I sit quietly in my bed or in my office. The world is quiet, and if it isn't, I stick a pair of earplugs in my ears. I imagine I am trading, and the market is moving against me. I see myself cut the loss.

I imagine I bought the XYZ, and I see it going my way. I feel the brain sending me signals to close the position to crystallise the profit. I see myself doing nothing, as I continue to watch the profit increase and decrease.

I see a big profit turn into a small profit. I smile and accept it, and I move on, telling myself it is okay. I place my brain under as much stress as I can with imagined scenarios. I am long and the market is going my way, and a sudden news story breaks the market.

Figure 23

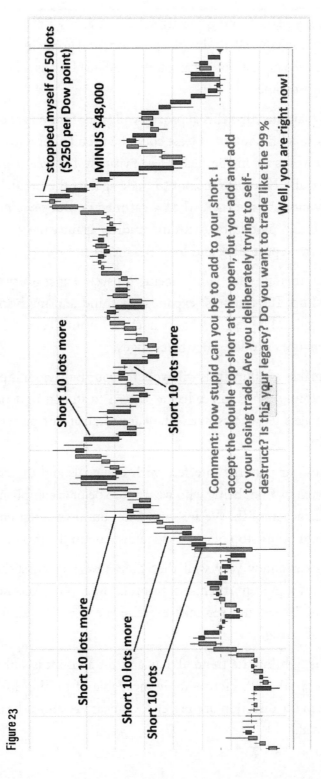

stopped myself of 50 lots
($250 per Dow point)

MINUS $48,000

Short 10 lots more

Short 10 lots more

Short 10 lots more

Short 10 lots more

Short 10 lots

Comment: how stupid can you be to add to your short. I accept the double top short at the open, but you add and add and add to your losing trade. Are you deliberately trying to self-destruct? Is this your legacy? Do you want to trade like the 99 %

Well, you are right now!

I observe my fear shooting through the roof as my P&L turns into a bloodbath. I see myself closing the positions and going in the opposite direction. I see myself not getting unhinged just because the market is moving against me.

I cannot guarantee that this approach will work for everyone. Perhaps you think it is brilliant, or at least could be useful after a few personal tweaks. It works for me because I learn visually. I *get the message* when I see it visually. If you *tell* me not to trade against the trend, it will not mean any more to me than when a cat meows. But *show* me a chart with my trades plotted on, with me trading against the trend (better yet, show me repeatedly), and I get the message.

This is my therapy. This is like seeing a psychologist every morning. I get fired up. The therapist expands my mind and my horizon. The goal is to remind myself of what behaviour I want to enact. It is about making changes and keeping the changes.

So what makes me think this will work for you? Behaviour is patterned. How we think, feel, and act has a pattern to it, and that patterning is what makes us who we are. The sum total of our patterns is our personality.

Sometimes our patterns interfere with our goals and dreams in life. They prevent us from being who we want to be or accomplishing what we want to accomplish. We are sometimes our own worst enemy, and we seemingly can't stop ourselves when we are in the moment.

A person can know very well that they have anger issues, and yet be unable to prevent themself from lashing out. Another might have eating issues, and yet can't exercise the needed restraint in the moment of eating.

A trader is fighting the trend all day and his account is suffering, but he can't stop himself. He is simply incapable of turning his position and trade in the direction of the trend. Only afterwards is he disgusted with himself.

The purpose of my warm-up is not to take away everything that is bad in our lives in one swift move. The purpose is not to guarantee I won't mess up. The purpose is to focus on what I want to achieve or become, while being mindful of the things that will most certainly sabotage my goals.

The wonderful part is that I am almost certainly guaranteed success if I avoid the failures. I was guaranteed success with my weight goal if I could cut out all the Coca-Cola I drank. I just had to be mindful of that, and the pounds began to come off. I didn't have to do anything else.

I don't have to be certain that my trade is going to work out. I just have to be aware that my mind wants to do things that are not in my own best interest. So, I don't add to my losing trades. That in itself means I just need to be mindful of the one variable I can control.

My action in the morning is about changing the patterns that do not serve me. This started by observing another very successful trader and asking myself what was holding me back from becoming him.

My technical abilities were just as good as his. I don't think he was financially much better off than I was, but he was seemingly fearless. How could I become fearless in trading? Did I even want to be fearless?

I came to the conclusion that the trader I wanted to become was patient but aggressive when the time was right. It was like Federer playing in the Wimbledon final in 2007: he was patient until just the right moment, and then played with focused aggression.

After that it was a question of reminding myself of that goal every day, and several times a day if necessary. That is how habits are built: through repetition.

As I grow wiser to the ways of life, I realise that there is a lot of truth to John Lennon's words, "Life is what happens to you while you're busy making other plans." We become so engaged in our day-to-day life, with responsibilities at work and home, that the big picture of our lives stays in the background.

Day after day, year after year we busy ourselves with work and routines, only to realise later in life that opportunities have passed us by. So, the first question to address in a change process is: "What do you want to change?" Or, stated otherwise: "How would you like your life to be different?"

My answer? I want to dedicate time to trading well, to combat my natural inclinations that stand between me and successful trading. I want to prepare my mind every morning through a series of meditations and visual exercises.

To achieve this I will train my mind to act calmly through visualising myself in difficult situations. I will focus on my breath. I will calmly put myself through stressful situations to ensure I would react how I want to react if the circumstances were real.

Making changes entails far more than simply engaging in positive thinking or getting positive images in your head. I didn't want positive images. I wanted a portrait of the dire hell I would reside in if I didn't change. This may seem like a negative state of being, but it really isn't. It is immensely positive, albeit a rather tense way of getting what you want.

As the saying goes: "The end justifies the means." I have turned conventional thinking on its head. I do so because I know what compels me more. Roses don't compel me. Thorns compel me to action.

Consider the market itself. It is not so unlike us in its behaviour (because we *are* the market). It climbs the wall of worry, but it slides down the slope of hope. It might be a Wall Street saying, but it says a whole lot more about humans than it says about the markets. All I have done is used fear and disgust as my protagonist – my major motivator.

GETTING BACK IN THE GAME

I was surfing in a town outside Biarritz, France, in 1996. I was literally in over my head. The waves were twice as big as anything I had ever handled before. I tried to drop in a few times, but the waves were too fast, and the lip was so steep.

Finally, I got myself positioned for a wave, but I was too far into the impact zone, and instead of gliding into the energy path of the wave, it literally knocked me out. I just remember everything going black. Luckily for me someone spotted me and pulled me out of the water. Eight lives left.

I was back in the water that afternoon. I was too stupid and ignorant to consider what had happened. Ignorance is bliss. It is only now that I can appreciate my behaviour. Sure, you took a hit, but you are okay. Do you want to sit on the beach and mope all day or do you want to get back in the game?

Here's an example illustrating the importance of getting back in the game.

I am writing this the day after a particularly challenging and volatile trading session. It was one of those days that will stick in your my mind for reasons that will shortly become apparent.

Over the last week oil has dictated the mood of the stock indices. Naturally, I expected to see the same behaviour on Friday. The Dow started off with a 200-point rally at the open.

However, 30 minutes into the trading session, it seemed to lose momentum. Oil on the other hand was in full-blown panic. I started shorting Dow, expecting it to follow oil.

In Figure 24, Dow is on the left, and oil is on the right. Both are five-minute charts, and both show the entirety of the trading session from about noon until late evening.

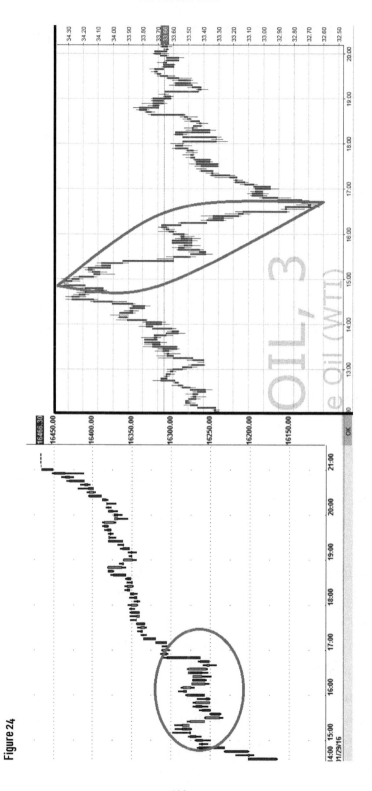

Figure 24

I expected the Dow to follow oil, and it did, but not for long. It seemed to pause, as if it suddenly had a mind of its own. By mid-afternoon oil had dropped almost $2 – more than 5% – in little over an hour. The Dow, however, wasn't moving lower with it. It held. I took my Dow short position off with a loss, and I reversed to long.

As soon as I had done that, the Dow dropped 50 points, and oil dropped even lower. I began to wonder if I had simply been too quick to reverse my position, and I decided to close my long position. By now I was convinced the Dow had merely delayed its inevitable fall. I went short again. In hindsight that turned out to be near the low of the day (after the open).

Just 15 minutes later the Dow made new highs for the day. I closed my short position and scratched my head. I had gone short at the first low and I had closed at the second high. I had gone long at the second high, and I had closed at the second low. I had gone short at the second low, and I had just stopped myself out at the new highs for the day.

I took a moment to reflect. Was I trading with a plan? Was I betting on a relationship between oil and the Dow Index that might not be there anymore?

Just then my best trader friend called, and we spoke briefly. I said to him, "What does it mean when the Dow makes new highs on a Friday evening, even though oil is plummeting?"

Saying it out loud helped me to get some perspective. It was the last day of the month, which often brings aggressive buying or selling in the market.

Remember it was also a Friday, which has a tendency to bring about trend days. I started buying, reluctantly. The market went higher. I bought some more, careful to move the stop-loss up as the markets moved higher. I kept an eye on oil. It was recovering nicely.

With 60 minutes to go (and no dinner), the Dow made a new high for the day; and I know from my statistics that you should not short a market that makes new highs for the day in the final hour.

By then I began to add more to my position. I was now betting on a classic trend day finish. On those days the market closes right at the high tick of the day.

It would have been easy to throw in the towel after the three failed attempts to get on board a move in the market. The effect would have been the same as stopping the game of throwing coins just because you have had three of a kind in a row.

I hear about people who stop trading because they have three losing trades in a row. That is a flawed approach if you understand the markets. If you are ill, or you are weighed down by emotional circumstances, then you stop trading. If you are otherwise able, you don't stop trading just because you have lost three times in a row.

As I type this, I look back at my trading before the Friday. I had lost on every other day that week. It is rare, but I had four losing days in a row. I don't even remember when that last happened.

In the movie *Floored*, the trader Greg Riba puts it so elegantly, albeit in his own way:

> I swear to god that 99% still don't get it. When they are winning, they start betting less. *Bet more.* I mean, if there is one roll that you can make a hundred thousand dollars on, let it ride. If you roll three sixes in a row, let it ride. Let the winners ride.

Greg Riba should know. He was said to be one of the best S&P 500 futures pit traders ever. Why do people bet less when they are winning and bet more when they are losing?

Fear.

TRADING THROUGH
A SLUMP

IHAVE A FRIEND who was suicidal because of the losses he sustained. He called me to say that he was standing at a railroad bridge. I don't think it was his intention to end his life. I think he needed someone to talk to.

Some would argue that a chapter of this nature does not belong in a trading book. I think people who have lost significant amounts of money will find it reassuring that the focus isn't one-sided.

Either way, while I have plenty of positive memories from my trading career, I also have memories that can only be described as *dark*.

I had a friend called Adam. I no longer know of his whereabouts. He owes me £20,000 – money I doubt I will ever see. Adam was a brilliant trader. Absolutely brilliant. Until it all unravelled for him.

Adam and his brother worked on the factory floor for their father's thriving business. During the 1990s Adam became interested in trading. Over the ensuing years he developed a system for trading stock indices using a 30-minute chart. He told me it was inspired in part by George Taylor's book *The Taylor Trading Technique*.

It was a simple but very effective strategy. It required Adam to check the charts every 30 minutes, and if the parameters were right he would execute a trade. Otherwise he would leave it alone until the next 30-minute period was up, at which point he would check the charts again.

Adam became so adept at trading the 30-minute chart that he soon made much more money trading than he did managing his father's factory. He decided to sell his share of the factory to his brother and focus all his energy on trading. Adam did well. Really well.

I traded with Adam on many occasions in my house or online. He possessed a supernatural patience. I have personally never seen a person stare at a screen from the open of the US market to the close of the US market and not trade once. Yet that was the norm for Adam if there was no signal.

Amazing patience.

I believe that Adam's patience and pattern-reading ability made him the supertrader that he was. He lived the life of the supertrader too. He ordered a custom-built house. He travelled first class to exotic holiday destinations with his loving wife and children.

However, all supertraders will go through bumpy terrain at some point or another. It is not a question of *if* it will happen – because it will – but a question of how badly it will affect them when it inevitably does.

For Adam the bumpy road caused him to lose everything. His trading account, his wife and his house. I stepped in when Adam was living on the streets in Manchester, suicidal and penniless. I did what I could – but Adam didn't want my help, and I lost contact with him.

It started with a bad loss, and it escalated into a complete blow-out. Adam had seen a pattern on a Friday night, and he had gone maximum short the market. At the close he was well in the money, and he decided to keep the position over the weekend.

Unfortunately for Adam, this was the weekend when the American special forces finally captured Saddam Hussein. The financial markets cheered at the good news. I guess naïvely they thought that the Middle

East powder keg would settle down once Saddam had been captured. That Sunday night the American markets opened *limit up*!

Limit up is a situation where the market is unable to move any higher until the stock market opens at 9.30 am in New York. Adam was short, but he was unable to close his short position because when the market is limit up you can't buy, which is what you need to do to close a short position.

Adam was awake when the phone call came. It was his futures broker. Adam was informed of his options: deposit more money on the account or risk being closed out once the future market came out of limit up. Adam didn't have any available capital. It was a long night and a long day until the market finally opened at 2.30 am (Adam lived in the UK).

The market opened and stocks soared. The broker liquidated his position because he was in breach of the margin requirement. The account had stood at close to £750,000. Now there was only £400,000 on the account.

You may say that £400,000 is also a decent pot of money to trade with, but something short circuited in his mind. He saw the market soar that day, and he saw his position being liquidated. Unfortunately, he also saw how the market came all the way back to his entry point.

You see, once the good news had been digested by the market, there was a feeling that this probably wasn't such great news after all. The Dow Index came all the way back, giving up all the gains for the day.

Adam felt the broker had cheated him. He felt as if he had been forced to liquidate. He felt that the broker had acted too hastily. He tried to complain, but his claim was rejected.

He then tried to make up for the lost money through trading, but his head wasn't right. He began to second guess his system and double up on trades. Then his builder demanded payment for his house. Adam had paid a deposit, but now he couldn't make full and final payment. He lost the deposit and the house.

Adam was unable to stop his own downfall. So was his family. He began a pattern of lying and withholding information for his own gain. The last time I heard from Adam was when he cheated me out of a fair sum of money, only to disappear. I haven't seen him since.

Sadly, this is not an isolated story. I have had to cut short a business trip while working in the London because my boss called me back to the office. There was a client in our reception crying his eyes out because he had lost £750,000 trading forex. He was afraid to go home and tell his wife about it. He begged my boss to lend him money so that he could trade again and hopefully make the money back.

You may think that this individual lacks the moral fortitude to trade. You may even think less of him because of his apparent lack of dignity. What if I were to tell you that he was a renowned surgeon in a prestigious private London clinic?

Education means very little in this industry. It doesn't matter where you went to school or what your day job is. If you don't know how to handle a losing trade, and then a winning trade, you will not go very far in this arena.

It is for this reason that I tell people to spend less time on technical analysis and more time on self-analysis.

Successful trading can mean just making a good living. I got a message from a close friend of mine. He trades full time. He has been doing it for 15 years and, unlike so many other hopefuls, managed to make a success of it. He has made himself a good living over the years.

I don't know many traders who like to talk about what they earn from their trading. When I spoke to my friend about it, he told me he had made about the same as if he had a well-paid managerial job in the City. However, he had no commute, and he had time to be there for his children when they came home from school.

To me, my friend is an example of a person who made trading work for him. He had not made himself rich in the process, but he had paid the bills, put food on the table for his family, taken them on holidays, and bought a nice family car.

There seems to be an inclination to describe trading as the venue for making untold riches. Yes, the potential is always there, but with bigger reward comes bigger risk. You can't catch big fish in shallow waters.

However, my friend was tiring from the long hours, and he called me to talk. He asked me if I had ever had enough of the endless hours of watching the screens.

I immediately responded, "No, and if you feel like that, you have to stop trading and take a break from it all." We spoke for a while that night on the phone.

He told me that now that the kids were older, they wanted to hang out with friends rather than their old dad. His wife worked full time too. It meant he was often alone in the house from early morning until later afternoon, and it began to bother him.

I helped him get a few job interviews and he secured himself a job as a broker in London, on account of his in-depth understanding of the markets and his ability to understand what clients are going through in their trading.

A fairly innocent story, I am sure you would argue; so why am I telling you about my friend? Well, I am telling you the story for several reasons.

The first reason is that trading can be a very lonely business. It has never bothered me, but I have the deepest of sympathy for those who feel lonely while trading. I am not sociable, don't drink or smoke, can't stand watching a football match (that excludes me from a lot of male social activities) and prefer my own company; but even I like to pick up the phone from time to time and just shoot the breeze with a friend.

When I worked in the City, I would at times stick my head into my boss's office, who always had a minute to say hi and catch up on life. If you one day decide to make a go of trading full time, you may experience a twinge of sadness that you no longer have the odd chat with a work colleague.

I recommend that you take a week or two's holiday and try full-time trading before you hand in your notice to your boss and begin your full-time online trading job. It will give you a taster of what your day will look like.

The second reason I told you the story about my friend is to make sure you realise that a pause from trading is not the end of trading. The markets will always be there.

My friend will no doubt be back to trading full-time one day. In the meantime, he is enjoying a new life where he is helping others achieve what they want from trading.

The third reason I am telling you this story is because I would love to see you succeed, but I think it is important you understand that trading may not offer you the rainbow you had hoped for. But does it have to?

Could it not just offer you a good income, where you are working on your own terms and perhaps doing something that you find immensely interesting? Does it have to result in owning a beachfront property in Barbados?

Sure, if you get there, I am happy for you, and you should be proud of yourself. However, if you don't get there, but you still manage to pay your bills and put money aside for the sweet things in life as if you were the recipient of a monthly pay cheque, then to me you have done what the 99% of the population do not dare to do.

They dare not take a chance on their dreams. If you can make a living from it, be it a decent living or a great living, then you really are something out of the ordinary.

And trust me when I say that once you understand trading better, you will also come to understand what makes you work optimally in the trading arena, and that is when being a trader gets really fun.

Eight months ago, I went through a tough time. It happened during the month of May. I started strongly, and then the wheels started falling off. I was up some £200,000 on the month, and it started to unravel.

It started with a loss of £33,000. Often when I have a bad day, I will come roaring back the day after, but I didn't. I lost another £9,000 the day after. Then came the weekend – not a moment too soon.

Monday started where Friday had left off, in spite of all my preparation and introspection over the weekend. I lost another £38,000. Before the week was over, I had lost more than 50% of the gains for the month.

More disturbingly, I felt completely lost. I had no idea why I was losing. I wasn't tired. I was sleeping well. I had no emotional issues that occupied my focus. I was just not performing.

I have endured hard times before. Progress has at times been slow. Setbacks have been frequent. Setbacks are always lurking. My goal is to stay in the game until I don't want to spend all my waking mental energy on the markets.

As you can perhaps gather, this is a deeply personal journey for me. It is often a mentally draining journey, where I feel I am not making any progress. What made it worse for me was that a really good friend of mine – also a trader, and probably the best private trader the world has never heard of – was having a great run.

We have always been brutally honest with each other. I think therein lies the strength of our friendship. I will tell him point blank, "I am jealous of you. I feel bad that I am jealous of you, because you are my closest friend, and I would give you my last dollar, but right now I am shooting blanks. I am haemorrhaging money."

I told him I had a huge position on. It was literally the biggest position I have ever carried. Each point was worth £4,000. That equates to 400 FTSE futures contracts. I was so certain the FTSE would fall.

I have seen the pattern so many times: big fall off the open – two to three bars of five-minute duration of rebound – and then new lows.

But it didn't. Not that day. It rallied. And he was long. I was short. It was immensely painful. It took me to a place I didn't want to visit. A place of envy, resentment and despair.

"You know Tom, you are lucky." My thoughts were interrupted by my girlfriend. It was as if she knew what I was thinking. "Not everyone has someone who is better than them, and who they stay up at night wondering how to beat. Not everyone is Mozart versus Salieri. You should be happy. So you lost. But what have you gained? Don't you know that he feels the same as you do? He desperately wants to beat you – for no other reason that you bring out the best in each other."

She carried on: "You know, my old professor Peele, I told you about him… brilliant man. Do you know what made him brilliant? His colleague – Professor Kyle – they were best friends and neither of them would ever acknowledge that they were insanely jealous of each other, yet they were the two most brilliant minds anyone could wish to learn from. You should really count your blessings that you have someone who you so badly want to beat. It is really not a curse. It is a blessing. What do you think would happen if your idols stopped trading?"

If they stopped, I thought, who would I beat then? I always loved beating my old high score, and I did today, in size; but she was right. I am not just trading to make money; I am trading to push myself into those places where I am not comfortable.

I was once in a restaurant in Porto Cristo, having dinner with my son. I happened to look over my shoulder and I saw Rafa Nadal having a late meal with his friends. It was great to witness a world-famous tennis star just shooting the breeze with his old friends.

A few days later we visited his tennis academy. Rafa was training. It was hot as Hell that day. He trained like his life depended on it. He was out there pouring his heart out – in the blazing heat – just to get better.

Why do you think he was doing that? It is for the same reason that someone like Matthew McConaughey – during his Oscar acceptance speech in 2014 – said, "There are three things that I need each day: one, I need something to look up to; two, I need something to look forward to; three, I need something to chase."

I am writing this because I think being open about what drives us is healthy. There will come a point in your career as a financial trader where you will go through a slump. When it happens, it might serve you well to step back and think deeply about why you are so drawn to this game.

And when it happens, I hope you will turn to these pages. I hope they will remind you why you are doing what you are doing.

What my slump taught me was to slow down. If you do not slow down and let the knowledge mature, then you will take a huge loss, which will dent your confidence.

Not every trade is the World Cup final. Not every trading session is the final exam of the final year, the culmination of four years of relentless studies.

Everyone has setbacks. Kobe. Rafa. Federer. You. Me.

And – all slumps end.

Slumps are inevitable. You are bearish and the market goes up. You are bullish, the market goes down. It happens to us all. Every one of us.

Is there a key to escaping a slump? No.

Why should I throw old, worn clichés at you? Why should I tell you to stay calm and work your way through it? Why don't I just tell you that it is horrible to go through, but it will end – if you persist?

I wrote this chapter over several weeks. When I started it, I was not in a slump. Then the slump arrived, and I described it. As I type these words, I have had a fantastic trading morning. Am I out of the slump? Who knows? I do not know what I am doing differently to what I did when the slump set in.

I am simply following the process I always follow. I am a process-oriented trader. The markets determine the outcome. I have little control over that. I have faith. I believe that my process will carry me through the highs and the lows of trading.

EMBRACING FAILURE

THE LATE MARK Douglas argued that successful trading is a question of accepting risk and thinking differently.

The Market Wizard trader Ed Seykota put it another way. "A losing trader can do little to transform himself into a winning trader. A losing trader is not going to want to transform himself. That's the kind of thing winning traders do."

When I read that passage the first time, I was not mature enough to understand its importance. When I started trading for myself, I began to appreciate its depth and wisdom.

As I began trading bigger and bigger size, I realised that my journey from a low-stakes trader to a high-stakes trader was not the result of evolution. Sure, I got better the more I traded, but remember this: Practice does not make perfect. It merely makes it permanent. Only through a dedicated approach to practice, with a specific attention to finding your mistakes, will you improve. Otherwise you just are just cementing your unprofitable behaviour.

BECOMING A DIFFERENT PERSON

Being anxious and fearful is a reflection of an unknown situation. Through exposure – over and over – our minds come to accept the new reality and through that exposure become accustomed to it.

You think there is a hack that will all of a sudden take you from trading £10 a point to £100 a point? You think there is some book you can read, or some course you can take, or a pill you can ingest that will take you from being an average-stake trader to a high-stake trader?

Well, not quite. But there are certainly ways you can accelerate your progress. It is a question of priority. I am not some hardcore monk with no life and a never-ending commitment to pushing myself into those cold, dark corners where I dance with uncertainty until my emotions are stunted and I essentially become a psychopath with no fear.

But I am committed. I want to explore my weaknesses. I am reasonably attuned to my mind and body, and I know that left to my own devices I can quickly spiral into self-destructive behaviour.

I had a painful breakup with a loved one, and I turned to food and alcohol. Sure, I think we all do things like that. Even Bridget Jones (I love movies) ate her way through a tub of ice cream in one sitting when she was dumped by the love of her life.

But you move on. You get off the sofa. You turn off the TV and throw the ice cream bucket in the bin, and you say, "Okay, so I made a mistake. I will own it."

How you feel about failure will to a *very* large degree define your growth and the trajectory of virtually every aspect of your life. You may want to close the book and think about that for a while. It is quite frightening how deep that sentence is.

A significant part of your success as a trader is correlated to your relationship with failing. If you see failure as the endgame, then you won't make it as a trader. I have colleagues who will stop trading if they have three losing trades in a row. What kind of attitude is that? You think Kobe Bryant – the absolute superman of basketball – had that attitude? You think during a game he would make three misses and then ask the coach to be replaced by someone else?

KOBE BRYANT – THE BIGGEST FAILURE

While we are on the topic of Kobe Bryant, I want to tell you a story about him, which I read in a paper – sadly after Kobe passed away in a tragic accident.

After the accident, most obituaries focused on Bryant's amazing achievements and trophies won, but Andy Bull from the *Guardian* wrote about Kobe Bryant from a different vantage point.

The headline of the article sums it up well: "Bryant's success story began with working to conquer the fear of failure."

It seems Kobe Bryant intuitively knew that, in order to be a great player, he needed to conquer his fear of failing. The article goes on to tell the story of a game in May 1997. It was Kobe's first season for the LA Lakers, his rookie season. He made four crucial errors inside five minutes, which some say cost his team the game.

That night, the story goes, Bryant stayed up shooting hoops privately and alone. He was still at it when the sun came up. I know this feels a little sugar-sweet; it has a David versus Goliath feel to it. But there is more to this than meets the eye.

On the surface, it reads that Kobe Bryant was beaten in that game and he followed it with a punishing all-night session. To me the story tells of a man who night-after-night confronted his fear of failure by repeatedly trying. He became used to sometimes failing temporarily, and yet he kept at it.

Bull concludes by saying, "He missed more shots than any other player in history. Bryant was willing to encounter failure in every game he played."

It is not the first story I have read about an all-American great, someone who confronted the fear of being wrong, in order to be proven right. Babe Ruth, the American baseball player, held home run records for decades. At the same time, he went by the nickname *King of Strikeouts*. If the term itself doesn't give it away, let me explain: a home run is great; a strikeout is the very opposite.

I found the story resonated with traders all over the world who seek out systems and strategies aimed at eliminating losing trades.

As I write this on a quiet trading day on 1 June 2020, I look over my trading statistics for the month of May. I made a total of 1,513 points. Yet out of the 137 trades I executed, I lost on 66 of them, won on 53 of them, and broke even on 18 of them (where stop-loss was moved to entry point).

If I gauged my success according to some of the hyped-up system sellers on the internet who promise a 95% (or better) hit rate on trades, I am an abject failure. I mean, I was less than 50/50 in May.

Yet, somehow, I still managed to make a decent return for the month. How do you explain that? The answer is found in the erroneous belief that the more winning trades you have, the better a trader you are. That is plainly and simply wrong.

One of the popular clichés in the trading world is that you can't go broke taking a profit. Oh, hell yes you can. If you are unable to let your profits run, you will never make money trading. While basketball and trading differ on this point, if I were afraid to lose, I would never have had a profitable month.

STATISTICS DO NOT MAKE SENSE

We know that 90% of traders lose. We also know from the FX trading sample of 25,000 traders that most trading accounts have more winning trades than losing trades. This does not make sense. How can we reconcile those two facts?

The answer is found if you read between the lines of the story of Kobe Bryant. If you are in a losing position, you are essentially wrong. However, unlike a shot in a basketball game, where you immediately know when you are right or wrong, in trading there is always the hope that the trade will come back in your favour.

Hope is what keeps people in trades long after they should have closed them. As the saying goes, *hope dies last*. So true, and so detrimental to traders. How do I deal with hope and fear in my trading?

I tend to only feel hope when I am in a trade. I hope my position will come good. I hope the market will move in my favour.

Fear, however, is felt in more situations. I can feel fear when I am in a trade. But I can also feel fear when I am not in a trade. That is a subtle but important distinction between hope and fear.

Hope tends to be reserved for the activity of being in the trade, while fear manifests itself both when I am in a trade and when I am not in a trade. I can be fearful that the market will move ahead without me, or I can be afraid that I have closed my position too soon – which could also rightly be classified as *regret*.

While I intend to write in much more depth about my trading regime at the end of the book, I will describe my approach briefly now.

I deal with fear when I am in a trade by having an exit strategy. I have a stop-loss, which defines the size of my loss. I have accepted this loss before I started the trading day. It is part of my trading plan.

I will have mentally prepared in the morning, ahead of the trading day. I will have sat quietly, contemplating what I am about to do. I will have subjected my mind to images of me losing. I will have calmed my mind, when it experienced these imagined losses, so as to negotiate away any feelings of anxiety and regret, as well as desires to get revenge and get even.

I will have dealt with hope by accepting that my stop-loss will define my exit. Maybe I will win. Maybe I will not win. Before the trading day started I will have gone through mental exercises that saw me enter the market, observe the market move against me, negotiate with my fear brain and the impulse urges it sent to my conscious awareness.

By the start of the trading day I will already have seen myself win and lose, add to positions, and patiently wait for the right setup. By the time the bell rings, opening the market for trading, I am mentally warmed up. I am ready to fail without losing my composure.

MY COMPETITIVE SON

I have a fascination with reading about the lives of high-performance soldiers. I love reading about the trials and tribulations of the SAS and Navy Seals. My son shares this interest. In particular, we are fascinated with the free-diving part of the training.

One of the obstacles that these elite warriors have to pass is the 50-metre underwater free-dive. Do you think there is a shortcut to diving 50 metres under water?

Take it from someone who has swum 46 metres under water, there is no shortcut. I practised and practised while on holiday with my son. There happened to a 50-metre swimming pool in the complex we were staying at.

Being the competitive spirits that both my son and I are, he set out first on our initial attempt. He made it a little less than halfway. Now I had a goal, and I made it almost to the halfway line. I beat him by an inch or two.

We spoke about how we could get better, and we agreed that we needed to focus more on our preparation before the swim. So next we sat on the edge of the pool, and we focused on filling our lungs with oxygen and oxygenating our bodies.

Gradually we got better and better. Then we realised that if we swam less frantically while underwater, we would expend less oxygen. Our focus shifted to staying calm and taking rhythmic strokes.

By the end of the seven-day holiday, I came within a few strokes of 50 metres. My son was a metre or two behind me. Passing this test is one of the major stumbling blocks for aspiring Navy Seals. I am not saying that my son or I are Navy Seal material, but I am saying that there is no way you are going to swim 50 metres under water without relentless practice.

We worked on it. Then we evaluated our process. We didn't actually focus on the outcome at all. We just did everything we could to make the process as efficient as possible. Does that remind you of something? If you have a goal that you want to make X amount of money a day, or a certain amount of pips or points, you might be sabotaging your chances of making a lot of money. You are outcome-oriented. You would benefit immensely from shifting your focus to being process orientated.

BEST LOSER WINS

THE TIME HAS come to get more specific. We can skirt around the issue forever, or we can decide to get our hands dirty and get down to the business of creating a finely tuned trading mind.

What you become in life is dependent on the decisions you make and how you react to decisions made on your behalf.

At Stanford University, Steve Jobs, standing at the podium in front of the class of 2005, gave the new graduates their commencement speech – advice on how to live life. It went something like this:

> Remembering that you're going to die is the best way I know to avoid the trap of thinking you have something to lose. You are already naked. There is no reason not to follow your heart.

Few can walk the walk when money is on the line. The main contributor to not having the life you want is fear. Most play this game called life safely within the boundaries they set while growing up, boundaries built by avoiding pain and anxiety.

I am often asked if I know the secret to becoming a good trader. I think many novices believe that I know some really good trading setups. They're not entirely wrong; yes, I know some great setups, but they still only work – at best – about 70% of the time. I am still wrong 30 times out of 100.

I am not where I am in the trading world because of my IQ. I'll tell you that immediately. I am here because of my relationship with pain.

Our brains hate the idea of losing something that is valuable to us. The brain will abandon all rational thought and make some really poor decisions trying to avoid losing something that has value.

I am a profitable trader. Is that because I possess superior charting abilities? No. Of course not. There are many brilliant chartists who can't trade.

Is it because I have a superior system? No, there are many great systems but most will still only have a 60% strike rate.

Is it because I have friends in high places that feed me insider information? No. Did you not read my book? I am socially reclusive, and I certainly do not have friends in high places.

I have no secrets. I have no special abilities, with the possible exception of one. Do you want to know why I am so good at trading?

I am exceptionally good at losing. When speculating in financial markets, *the best loser wins*. Don't underestimate these four words.

Though it may go against the conditioning that life and the modern world have programmed you with, success in financial market speculation is not about being the best, coming first, or winning.

Instead, it's about losing. Your relationship with fear and adversity will to a very high degree define your life.

And that's why I win. I win because I'm really good at losing. In trading, unlike life, it's the best loser that wins. Do you think a dentist, or a doctor would be in business if they had a 60% win rate? Of course not. But a trader can thrive and prosper on that kind of success rate – as long as they are prepared for it. Most are not.

MANY ARE CALLED...

Trading attracts many people who shouldn't be traders. They are led to believe that trading is easy. Maybe a broker is tempting them; I'm sure you've seen the broker advertisements where a calm, confident actor knowingly pressing buttons in front of a bedazzling array of screens, then walks away victorious with a confident smirk.

If you look at the trading industry, we are led to believe it is all about the tools. Hang on – do you think I can play tennis like Roger Federer just because I have a Wilson Pro tennis racket?

It's an illusion. How do I know? Because, for years, I was an insider working at one of the largest financial market brokers in London.

Why do so many people lose? Statistically speaking, it should be impossible for so many people to lose. If the market is random – and most of the time, market movement is indeed random – why do 90% of clients consistently lose a 50:50 bet?

The answer is as simple as it is complex. It isn't the market-beating them. They are beating themselves. I wasn't always a successful trader either. To become successful, I had to break down the barrier that separates the many from the few, in a business where there is no instruction manual, and where the lesson comes after the test.

It didn't take me long as a broker to notice our clients' trading behaviour. As a group, traders are predictable. Or, more accurately, their outcome is predictable, because everyone is doing the same thing.

I watched thousands of traders execute millions of trades. Their behaviour became predictable, almost as if they were connected together in one hive mind. Week after week, month after month, year in, year out, when they were making a loss they hoped the market would give them back their losses, yet when they were making a profit they feared the market would take it away.

They were fearful when they should have been hopeful. They were hopeful when, in fact, they should have been fearful.

These human experiences helped make me the trader I am today. Watching them struggle, I realised they were searching in the wrong place.

The answer they were so desperate to find is not found in the external. It's not found in the software, or in any of the tools. Instead, I realised, the answer is to be found inside the self.

TUNING MY MIND

In the silence of the early morning, I'm in my office, preparing for the day's trading. It is a minimalistic office. Depending on where I am, there are either two or four screens. That is it. There are no special monitors or water-cooled PCs.

My secret ingredient is a couple of files on my hard drive. There is my PowerPoint presentation on one screen. There is a Microsoft Word document on another.

The PowerPoint file is my cue. At game time, before I begin to trade, it's time to become someone else. In the movie *Gladiator*, why does Maximus Decimus Meridius rub dirt on his hands before combat?

It's a ritual.

He must immunise himself before battle, to feel nothing, to become an instrument of death, indestructible, so that he can survive another day.

Rubbing dirt on his hands is his ritual of leaving his old self behind. Every day from 5 am until 9 pm, even late into the night, I am battling myself. Trading is a battle of the self.

The PowerPoint file contains old trades, mistakes, triumphs, inspirations, and warnings visually arranged to prepare me for the day ahead.

I need to become something else; otherwise, I will not make money. This is why trading looks simple when looked at from the outside, but it's not easy because trading successfully goes counter to virtually every piece of DNA stored in your body.

In the 1960s, neuroscientist Paul MacLean proposed the human brain has evolved with three areas of function: the reptile brain, the limbic brain, and the neocortex.

So, who's really in charge when you are trading?

It's your reptile brain, your base self, that's really in charge. When you are startled, and you react, perhaps you detect a wobble in your stomach, a vibration in the lower back – that's your reptile mind preparing you for survival, triggering a fight-or-flight response.

Will you run, or will you fight? Your subconscious reptile mind has only one function, and that is to protect you. It does this whether you want it to or not.

And this is a problem, because to be successful as a trader you need to be very good at losing. This means constant conflict with your built-in subconscious protection system.

A system that protected you from death as a caveman guarantees you'll not survive as a trader – unless you can learn to overcome it. And overcoming it begins with accepting pain.

One exercise I use in the morning is closing my eyes and playing out a scenario. I imagine I lose a large amount of money. I will often use an amount that has some significance to me, such as the cost of my last car, or the cost of my son's college tuition, or the size of a memorable loss.

Say for the sake of the argument that I have opted to meditate on losing £78,000. I will see myself losing the amount. I will let it sit there – in my consciousness. I will let it take hold. I will imagine what I will not be able to buy because of the loss. I will make it as emotionally vivid as I can.

Now I will turn the table. I will now imagine that I am winning the same amount. I will imagine that I am winning the £78,000. What will happen is that my emotional response system *will not allow me* to feel a reciprocal sense of joy to the misery I felt earlier.

Neurobiology has shown we experience a financial loss 250% more intensely than an equivalent financial gain. After going through this exercise of feeling pain and then *not* feeling pleasure, I then swap back to feeling the loss again.

The purpose of the exercise is to align my feelings of gain and loss. In truth, I don't really want to feel anything – I have found that if I get overly happy about a win, I tend to get overly sad about a loss. I don't want that.

I am not a dentist who has a win rate of 99.99%. I am a bloody trader, who has to live with being wrong around 50% of the time. It is exhausting to feel joy and pain many times a day. I prefer not to feel anything at all, rather than going through that emotional roller coaster.

I win. Move on.

I lose. Move on.

By adopting this attitude and by warming up my subconscious mind, I am able to flow in and out of winning and losing trades, day in and day out, without it affecting my strategy.

Pain is inevitable to some degree in life. Someone lets you down, you feel pain. Someone hurts you emotionally or physically, you feel pain.

In life, outside of trading, one way to deal with the pain is to talk to someone. As the saying goes, *a problem shared is a problem halved.*

Why a painful experience feels less potent after we have shared it with a friend I don't know. Maybe the act of verbalising the disappointment puts the problem into a healthier perspective.

Either way, you feel better, and the pain subsides.

But when I'm trading, while the majority look to run away and rid themselves of pain, I do the opposite. I run towards it. I embrace it. I don't want to share my pain. I want to hold on to it. I need it.

Whether you are new to trading and speculation, or you have years of experience, you should give this question some serious thought:

If you want to be a success in a field where 90% or more fail, how do you think you should approach this task?

Trading looks easy on the outside, but in reality it's much more challenging than people expect – because we are hardwired to do the opposite of what we should be doing. This is why 90 out of every 100 people end up losing.

The road to consistency, success, and enlightenment in trading begins in the last place you'd ever think to look. Inside yourself.

THE KEY

So, here it is. What follows is the key that will unlock the door to your success, the key to breaking down the barrier between the life you want and the life you are leading now.

If you want to succeed in an endeavour where 90% are failing, you have two choices. You can study the large 90% losing group and do the opposite of what they do, or you can replicate what the 10% do.

If you are not as successful as you want to be, sooner or later you need to change your behaviour. It doesn't matter if you've been trading unsuccessfully for three months or 30 years, you are much closer to success than you realise.

The 90% fail because they interpret the pain messages received automatically from our reptile brain without any modification.

You need to learn to recode your brain's messages when pain comes knocking. Instead of reacting and running away, a small group of consistent traders, the 10%, hold fast and run towards the danger – not away from it.

The 10% succeed because they have learned to flip the switch.

FLIP THE SWITCH

This will feel very uncomfortable, but it is a discomfort you must accept and embrace if you want to succeed in the game of financial speculation. It is the reason why trading looks simple but is not easy.

The paradox of trading is this: by doing what the 90% cannot do, you will become successful. In other words, I *expect* to be uncomfortable. I expect my trading to cause me anxiety. I am waiting for it.

I can sum it up in a few sentences:

1. I assume I am wrong – until proven otherwise.

2. I expect to be uncomfortable.

3. I add when I am right.

4. I never add when I am wrong.

ASSUME YOU ARE WRONG

Remember, I've watched thousands of traders execute millions of trades, and I noticed when most traders enter into a position they assume they are right. In a business where 90% of people fail, your recoding process begins by flipping that switch.

I will assume that I will quickly have to get rid of a losing trade. My confidence in this action is not centred around my ability to select the right setup. That is what the 90% will do.

Instead, my confidence is centred around trusting I will get rid of a trade that is not performing. I trust myself to know that if this trade does not work out, there will be another one coming shortly.

Do you see how I have flipped the switch on my thinking? I am thinking differently to the 90%. I will assume I am wrong until the market proves me right.

Flip the switch!

When the 90% of traders execute trades, they experience emotions, which originate from their pain centre. Now it's only a question of time before their emotionally driven pain threshold centre sends them a false signal, causing them to lose. It is a never-ending rollercoaster ride of disappointment, lost money and pain.

When I trade, I assume I am wrong. I enter a trade, and the trade moves in my favour. I am trading my account size or the available profit – I am trading the market because I understand the size of my profit is irrelevant to the market.

I know my P&L has no influence on the market. I know that my brain's automatic pain receptor will kick in causing an inbuilt safety reflex to register pain.

I am subject to the same built-in automatic pain receptor as everyone else, but the difference lies in how I handle the pain. Instead of giving in to it, instead of being ruled by my emotional responses, I have flipped the switch. I have trained myself to expect the pain.

I am aware of the pain. It is there. It is real, but I accept it. I have encountered it in training over and over. It no longer acts as a debilitating force in my life. I have trained the fear of out my decision making.

EXPECT TO BE UNCOMFORTABLE

How can you have a good time while you are uncomfortable? Logic will say it is not possible. Well, for starters, I think all humans come alive when we strive. We toil in the garden, we work out, we study for an exam. I think it *is* perfectly possible to be uncomfortable while enjoying a challenging process. As a trading position grows in profit, instead of giving into the fear it will be taken away from me, I flip the switch, using my mental warm-up, my training exercises and visualisation of trend days where the market just goes higher and higher all day.

I flip the switch in my mind from negative mental imagery to positive mental imagery. I see myself riding this monster momentum wave. I see myself being at the forefront of every tick higher.

The 90% will focus on what they want to avoid. I focus on what I want to achieve. The 90% give in to their fears. I expect my fears to come in abundance, and I have a plan for counteracting them. I see a different image.

And when I am losing?

Well, I already expected to lose anyway, so the market disagreeing with my trade will not be associated with pain or fear. I expected it. I have accepted my loss already.

I don't entertain the idea of compounding my mistake by adding to my losing position. I have trained that trait out of my mind. It doesn't even enter my mind anymore. My mind knows I want to be big when I am right, and I want to be small when I am wrong.

Emotions kill trading accounts. It isn't the lack of knowledge that's stopping you from winning big. It's the way you handle yourself when you are in a trade.

I spent a decade observing traders lose money. They were intelligent people who often had great hit ratios, but they couldn't lose well.

After reading this far, if you remember only one thing, remember this: in trading, unlike life, the best loser wins.

THE IDEAL MINDSET

THERE IS AN ideal way to think as a trader. There is an ideal mindset – one that is flexible to the extreme. It does not care about winning. It does not care about losing. It is a carefree state of mind, but it still acts in your best interest.

The ideal trading mindset has no fear. If you are alarmed by this statement, then pause for a second. The ideal mindset may have no fear, but the ideal mindset is still acting in your best interest. The ideal mindset might be fearless, but it is not reckless.

Fear plays a significant role in explaining why people lose the game of trading. This fear can manifest itself in several ways. It can be the fear of not being in the market and missing a good move. It can be the fear of staying in the market for too long and seeing the open profits disappear.

Can you acquire an ideal mindset? Yes. Without a doubt. You may have to grow into it. You may have to begin a period of significant introspection and get to *know thyself*. I will discuss how to get to know yourself as a trader shortly.

The ideal trader mindset does exist, and you can train yourself towards this state of thinking and believing. When you arrive at this state, it means you are able to perceive information from the markets without feeling threatened or fearful.

Does it mean you will never lose? No. You will have losing trades just like everyone else. However, the ideal trading mindset is as at peace with losing trades, as it is with winning trades. Neither will impact your ability to unemotionally and dispassionately perceive market information in a non-threatening frame of mind. Your emotional state will stay in balance.

Every trader has experienced periods of being in the zone, of being balmed by the soothing feeling of the ideal mindset. It often happens when certain circumstances are present. For me personally, I experience that sense of calm whenever I am trading while on holiday.

One story stands out. I was on holiday for 14 days, and I traded every day from my holiday home. I was totally at peace, trading only when the market really spoke to me. Otherwise, I was at the pool relaxing in the sun.

When I returned to the trading floor, my boss came out and said, "Someone is on fire!" and clapped. Fourteen days later I had given away all my holiday profits. I remember the story so vividly because it happened to be one of the catalysts that led me to seek a deeper understanding of myself as a trader.

HARD-CODED DNA

The ideal mindset does exist, but few traders have it consistently. When we do not operate from a frame of mind of the ideal mindset, we are afraid of something. This fear is a manifestation of a lack of trust. We do not trust ourselves to do what we have to do without hesitation, without reservation or internal conflict or argument.

Our mind is the problem. Our mind's core objective is to keep us alive and avoid pain. We are automatically wired to think in a way that keeps us alive. This thought pattern is hard-coded into our DNA. It might keep us alive, but it makes trading difficult.

The very thing that keeps us alive is the very thing that makes trading an incredibly difficult proposition, until you have learned how to counter your hard-coding.

The issues we face largely fall into two categories:

1. We associate *this* moment with *another* moment, whether we are conscious of it or not.

2. We have a mind wired to avoid pain.

We have learned to *associate* in order to benefit from experiences. Association (connecting past moments with the present moment) and pain avoidance do not go hand in hand with trading.

Why do I say this? Why do I say that association and pain avoidance are detrimental to profitable trading? I say so because in trading each moment is unique, and anything can happen. Trading is the equivalent of a coin-flip game. Since the win ratio of many professional traders – including myself – is not far from 50/50, the coin-flip analogy is even more appropriate than you might think.

If you play a game of heads and tails, you are probably not too concerned about the outcome. Over time it will play itself out quite predictably. You will win 50%. You will lose 50%. If you developed a system where you lost a unit on your losses, and you made 1.5 units on your wins, you have yourself a good business.

Trading is just like that in many respects. You don't judge your system on the merit of one trade. You judge it over many trades. We do so because even a game of heads and tails will show an uneven distribution, even if the outcome over 100 flips is 50/50. As my friend David Paul once said, "There is randomness in the outcome of one, but there is order in the outcome of 100." He was talking about the coin-flip scenario.

I once flipped a coin 100 times, and I wrote down the result on a piece of paper. I witnessed 15 heads in a row. At one point I stopped and looked at the coin, as if to see whether there were obvious flaws to it. There weren't. If you had 15 losing trades in a row, I imagine your mental state would suffer. If you had 15 winning trades in a row, you may feel invincible.

The market will do what the market will do. It doesn't care about you or your position. It doesn't care if you are in the market or on the side-lines. If you have 15 winners in a row, it doesn't care. If you have 15 losers in a row, it doesn't care.

You can't make the argument that just because you have lost on a trade you are now closer to winning. By doing so, you are doing exactly what we need to learn not to do. Every moment is unique. Just because you had 15 heads in a row does not mean the odds of a head are less on the 16th throw. They are still 50/50.

Why? Because there is complete randomness in the outcome of one. That is another way of saying that every moment is unique. However, over time the law of averages will come into play, and over 100 throws, you will experience 50 heads and 50 tails.

However, while you may understand this academically, and even logically, there is a good chance you will not understand this emotionally, especially if you just had 15 winners or 15 losers in a row. Therein lies the difference between the trained mind and the untrained mind. I will steadily guide you towards the trained mind, so that you do not succumb to fear.

PERCEIVING INFORMATION

Information on its own has no power over us. It is our belief system and the energy we give to the information that decide its potency. If you receive an email from an unknown person saying, "You are a dead man," the chances are your emotional reaction will be very different than if you received an email saying, *"Du er en død mand."*

The message is the same. One is in English, the other Danish. On its own, the sentence is merely a construct of letters put together. Once it is decoded by the brain, it is assigned an emotional charge. The sentence is meaningless. It is how we interpret the sentence that causes the emotional response.

So, imagine a mindset where you can perceive the market information *purely* from an opportunistic point of view. You are not threatened by the information. You are not thinking, "Oh God, why am I not in this move?" You are not thinking, "Why am I in this move?" You merely observe and decide from a frame of mind that sees opportunities. It does not see threats.

The market moves up and down in *ticks* all day. They form patterns, which we trade on. These ticks up and down are just ticks. If you have a position on, however, these ticks take on a life and meaning of their own. They validate you, or they diminish you. That is not how you want to trade. That is not an ideal mindset.

FOCUS AND ATTRACT

What we focus on is what we attract. I believe in that, so it is true for me. The fear we experience causes us to focus on the object of our fear so that we end up creating the very experience we're trying to avoid.

I want to give you a simple example of the mind seeking information as a result of what your focus is on. You bought yourself a new car. It is a yellow Volkswagen Beetle. As you drive your new car, you begin to notice other Volkswagen Beetles. You never did that before. Your mind has opened a filter, allowing information about Beetles into your consciousness.

What we focus on is what we attract. The trader who has a position on in the market will focus on the price movements (the ticks) that move in his or her favour because they relieve pain and give pleasure. Movements against the position create pain.

You might be thinking I am stating the obvious. You are right. My point was not to state the obvious, but to point out that this state of mind is not open to other possibilities. The more fear we experience, the less information the mind will focus on. It will narrow its focus. It will stop you from perceiving alternative options.

I run a live trading channel, where I trade in real time. When I trade publicly, one type of scenario I am most proud of is that in which I accept I have misread the market, and I change my position. For example, I may have pushed the short side on the Dow Jones Index, and the market is moving against me. I accept I am wrong. I close my position. I open a trade in the opposite direction.

It requires a tremendous amount of self-belief to do this when you are trading big size. What helps me in situations of this type is to recite a mantra I have created: "Focus on the process. Focus on what you can control." I have developed a belief system that allows me to encourage this kind of flexibility.

This kind of mindset is possible for you too. When I set out, I wanted to create a mindset that allowed me to perceive information without fear. That is the ideal mindset. It takes time to create it, but your rewards are directly correlated to your effort. Don't expect a eureka moment. Expect to get better and better gradually.

BELIEFS

Our beliefs determine how we react to information. We were born with a clean slate, and our beliefs are taught and adopted. We were taught what to think. We also had experiences that shaped our beliefs.

I will get personal for a second. I felt my mother and father abandoned me at a young age. They divorced and I became the object of their fighting. I see now how that shaped my beliefs, which in turn influenced my choices in life and the decisions I made. The moment I was old enough to take charge of my own destiny, I saved up as much money as I could so that I could say goodbye to that toxic environment and leave my home country.

How does this relate to trading? Trading gives us unlimited potential to express ourselves. We can open a trading account, and away we go. You are your own boss. There are no rules. There are no limits. Do what you want. You are no longer influenced or guided by your parents. The world is your oyster. You have total freedom to do what you want to do, when you want to do it.

We tend not to want to operate under rules. After all, much of our young adulthood is spent rebelling against parents giving us rules. Trading is a rule-free environment. Unfortunately, the result is quite astounding. Traders have free will, and 90% of them will have a belief system that leads them to failure.

In order to prosper in trading, we need a combination of being able to operate under trading rules while not feeling we are being held back, because ultimately, we want to experience total freedom. Essentially, what it boils down to is creating a mindset that always acts in your own best interest. It is a mindset that allows you to see opportunities. It knows your weaknesses and what to be mindful of. It allows you to receive information without being threatened by the information.

You can operate from a carefree state of mind. I have created a blueprint for a carefree trading mind. I have changed my beliefs about trading. That is the message at the heart of this book – to change how we think, especially how we think about losing. It is to explain my mindset and teach you the mindset.

The old way of thinking is still there. It will always be there. It is part of your personality. But the old belief has no charge anymore. It is faded, diffused. Just because you have said goodbye to an old belief does not mean it isn't still in your memory.

I will give you a childish example. We used to believe in Santa Claus. We used to believe if we were good, he would come and visit us to leave us presents. Does it bother you that he is not real? Of course not. You have diffused the emotional charge of being deceived. Your life is no worse off. I have the same sentiment about my old trading beliefs. I am not missing out. I am thriving on a new mindset. I used to think I couldn't live without a cigarette after a meal. Now I can't imagine a life where I stick a cigarette in my mouth. I eat every day, and I never have an urge to smoke. Once I could not imagine a life without a smoke. Now I can't believe I was ever hooked on it. It took me a little more than a week to re-program my mind. The same will happen to you as you apply my blueprint for the ideal trading mindset.

My biggest belief I had to overcome in trading was the associations I made when I was confronted with losses. I had to learn how to disassociate losses from feelings of failure or feelings of wanting to extract revenge on the market to create a state of mental equilibrium. Achieving that was a momentous leap for my trading performance.

THE *BOOK OF TRUTHS*

I want to move the narrative towards the practical element of creating the right mindset. You can only dance around the fire for so long. Let's get down to brass tacks. Let's get specific.

I once saw a sign that said, "The best views come after the hardest climbs." Proverbs have a way of simplifying complex messages, but they are hit-and-run in their nature. They don't tell you *how* to do it.

How do I climb the mountain? Telling us to "Just Do It" might be well intentioned, but falls disastrously short of a meaningful description of how to climb the damn mountain. In a similar vein, to be told to just "run your profits" and "cut your losses" falls disastrously short of providing a meaningful guide to achieving these noble trading goals.

When I started trading, I had the right credentials. On paper I was academically destined to do well. Emotionally, though, I was like everyone else. I was not making money. I should say I wasn't making meaningful money. I lost more on bad days than I made on good days. Granted I had more good days than bad days, but the bad days would set me back significantly, to the point where I might as well go and get a job. It would have paid better than my trading did.

I didn't question what I brought to the game beyond chart preparation. I showed up. I traded. I studied charts. That was it. I thought that was all there was to it. If it didn't go well, then I had to do more of it.

However, I never looked inwards. Then something happened. I read the research (described earlier in the book) on the 25,000 traders executing 43 million trades, and I thought to myself, *I am just like them.* They all believed they would be profitable. Practically none of them were.

It prompted me to start thinking about trading holistically. I had been obsessed with techniques. I had a belief that *more is better* when it came to technical analysis. Yet, I was not seeing the results I wanted.

It got me thinking about *thinking* and about what I believed. More importantly, I began to wonder if what I considered to be my beliefs were actually helping me to become a better trader. So far, they had not.

Your beliefs create your world. How you see the world is a result of what you believe in. Some beliefs are easy to identify. I believe we should look after the environment, so I make sure I recycle. That is an example of a belief. That was an easy example. How are your beliefs shaping your trading performance? Are you even aware of what your trading beliefs are?

Your trading performance is a function of your belief system, and only by dissecting your trading performance are you able to uncover what your belief system is. There is an easy way to discover your trading beliefs. Although I say it is easy, it is also hard work.

A friend of mine wanted to improve his surfing, so he hired a friend to video him for a few hours during a surf session. He watched himself surf and he was able to identify his issues. He needed to strengthen his core muscles and he needed to trust his wave selection rather than being half committed, as he often was on many waves.

In a similar way, I decided I needed to relive my trades to truly figure out what my problem was. So, I downloaded my trading results into an Excel spreadsheet and went to work. I meticulously went through the trades. I split my trades up into many different categories, with many of them appearing in more than one category.

There were trades I held for days. There were trades I held for seconds. There were trades I executed in the mornings. There were trades I executed in the afternoons and evenings.

I recommend you read my assessment of my own trading, and you repeat it on your own trading. It is a vital step in understanding who you are and how you interact with the markets. Once you have done that, you will create what I call the *Book of Truths*.

Above all, be honest with yourself, as I was. If you are not honest with yourself, you will not be rewarded with consistency in trading. The courage to be honest with yourself is its own reward.

Here goes:

1. I had periods where my win rate exceeded 85%.

2. My average profitable trade was less than my average losing trade.

3. I was a winning trader, but my big losses were seriously denting my overall P&L.

4. I traded well in the first half of the day.

5. I traded well in the first three to four days of the week.

6. I often gave away much of my profit from the morning session when I traded in the afternoon.

7. I often gave away much of my weekly profit on Fridays.

8. I would do very well on range-bound days.

9. I would almost always miss trend days, and I would often fight them.

10. My biggest losses came from fighting trending moves.

The breakdown of my performance was incredibly cathartic. I took great pleasure in reviewing my own mistakes, because it felt like I was actually meaningfully moving towards a better version of myself.

I took a very time-consuming decision to put all of my trades on the relevant charts. I created a PowerPoint containing every trade to give me visual imagery of my performance. This is the *Book of Truths*.

I will argue that this process stood out as the single most beneficial practical exercise in enhancing my performance. I was, and I am, confronted daily with all my flaws, and I have a visual representation of those flaws. It seems as if the act of portraying a loss in a visual representation is a much more powerful tool for change than merely writing "Don't trade without a stop-loss" on a Post-It Note and taping it to your screen.

I use the PowerPoint file to warm up every morning before trading begins. I am reminded of the things I am good at and the things that tend to be my downfall. It has become an integral part of my process, to ensure I am acting in my own best self-interest.

When I started the process of visually recalling my old trades, my old hurts, my old successes, I felt an empowering surge to replicate what I was good at and avoid what I was bad it. I immediately began to trade differently. I immediately saw measurable improvements in my trading. The results were immediate, even if I had to get used to the new way of thinking. I made more money.

I became much more trusting of the markets. I trusted that I would be given an opportunity to make money every day. As odd as it sounds, I began to trade less, and I started to make more money. Sure, I wasn't perfect from day one. I am not perfect today either. In fact, one of my beliefs is *don't insist on perfection in trading*.

One truth I came face to face with was *less is more*. There was a clear relationship between the time of the day and my profitability. I was nowhere near as profitable in the afternoons as I was in the mornings. Would I make more money if I just traded mornings? The statistics said yes. My heart said no. I wanted to trade, and I felt (or rather my belief dictated) I had to trade in the afternoons. How else could I call myself a trader if I only traded part time? It was a process of trial and error.

This was the immediate benefit from the *Book of Truths*, but I didn't stop there. I began to seriously question my motivation for trading. I argue that in a business like trading, where 90% fail to make a positive return on their trading account, the only way to separate yourself from the masses is to acknowledge that your mind is either your best friend or your worst enemy.

If you don't prepare your mind ahead of the game, and you experience adversity during the game, your mind will most likely work against your prime objective. Your prime objective is *not* to make money. Your prime objective is to follow the strategy you have developed. More importantly, your prime objective is to follow the *process* you have designed for yourself. If you follow the process, the outcome will take care of itself.

I don't set goals. I just focus on my process. I am a process-oriented trader. I don't think being overtly goal oriented will help you achieve your goals. Of course, the goal is to win. But a mind subjected to adversity is a mind in stress. A stressed mind needs structure and process. Otherwise, it will succumb to feelings of fear, revenge and desperation, and the decisions it makes will originate from these feelings. Who wants to make decisions about the wellbeing of their financial health based on fear or stress?

The mind needs guidance. I read about an American football coach who, during the half-time break, gave specialised talks designed to re-awaken the imagination of the players on his team. One time his team had taken a beating in the first half of the game. During the break in the locker room the coach put on a special video he had prepared. It showed some of the greatest comebacks in football history.

The purpose of the video was to give the players a path out of their stressed state. It gave them mental imagery of what was possible. Coupled with the right kind of motivation, encouraging the players to focus on the process, staying present in the moment, waiting for the right opportunity and trusting the process, their minds had gone from being stressed to being prepared.

I want to remind you that the first part of my trading life was spent on a trading floor, observing traders – thousands of them – go about their daily lives. I am adamant in my claim that those who were behind at half-time had no mental tools to help themselves, and as a result tended to dig the hole they were in deeper and deeper, as the day wore on.

LEAVING THE OLD SELF

Remember how Maximus ritualistically rubs dirt on his hands before combat in the movie *Gladiator*? How, through this symbol of mental preparation, he was leaving his old self behind? Well, I too have to leave my old self behind. I too have to become someone else for the day. Charlie Di Francesca, the legendary bond trader in the pits in Chicago, said that good trading goes against normal human instinct. To succeed you have to get used to being uncomfortable.

Trading is a battle of the self. Every morning I have to shed my skin and become someone else. The *Book of Truths* is key to my transformation. It arouses a desire to do better than the old pattern of behaviour. I am certain that had I not taken the steps to focus on my mental game and confront myself daily with my old behaviour, I would not be where I am today.

I argue this to be the case based on my observations of diaries. One of the catalysts for my trading transformation came from tidying up my old office cabinets. I found old trading diaries in which I had meticulously described my trading day. As I read through the diaries, which spanned a decade, I saw how desperate I was to make trading work for me.

I saw how day after day I promised myself not to add to losing trades – how I promised myself not to trade well from Monday to Thursday and then lose it all on Friday – how I promised myself I would stick to one setup, and so on.

As I read page after page of trials and tribulations (but mostly trials), I realised that the Tom whose words I was reading was in real pain, but he was not transforming. He was repeating the same mistakes day after day. He might have been increasingly technically competent, as his studies took him deeper and deeper into expert territory of technical analysis, but he kept making the same mistakes when his mind became stressed.

As I have said before, it was not an epiphany. My change came slowly. It was a gradual realisation that all my chart studies didn't move me meaningfully towards the goals I wanted to accomplish. Rather, they merely distracted me from the real problem, which was my behaviour when things did not go to plan. Instead of focusing on the process and having tools to get me to operate from a stress-free mind, I succumbed to foolish trading, intending to make back the lost ground. My mind desperately wanted to get rid of the pain of having lost money, and its solution was to chase every movement in the market recklessly. And all I did was dig the hole deeper and deeper.

The *Book of Truths* will give you up-close, face-to-face time with your own shortcomings. It made me realise what my faults were. I also started plotting my good trades. I felt it was necessary not just to remind myself of the behaviour I wanted to avoid. I should also remind myself of the behaviour I wanted to strive towards.

The charts I use to prepare for each trading day, to warm up, are my old trades plotted on a chart. That way I can emotionally relive the trades and reinforce the behaviour that is good for me and remind myself what my weak points are.

AN EXAMPLE

Friday 4 March 2022 was an extremely volatile trading day. A colleague pointed out to me that Brent Oil was soaring. I looked at the chart, shown in Figure 25, and I thought, "Wow, it really is."

I bought the first retracement on this ten-minute chart. Now there is nothing wrong with this entry. I am trading *with trend*, but as I look back at the trade, I acknowledge that at that precise moment in time I was not trading from an emotionally stable point of view. I was eager to get on board a move, based purely on the opinion of another trader.

So, I just bought it without much thought to it. And I had no stop loss in mind. I just put an arbitrary stop loss, for safety. See Figure 26.

Figure 25

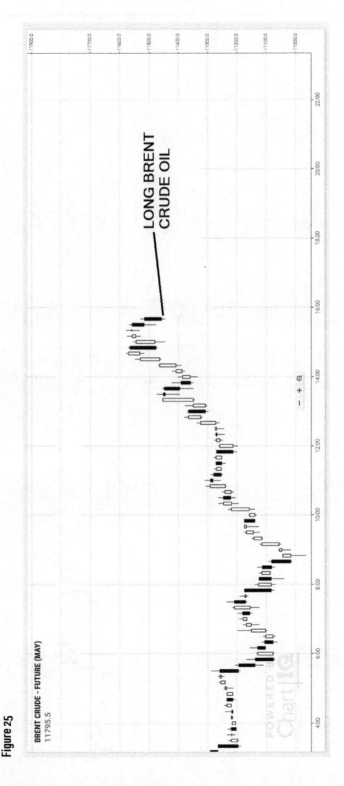

BRENT CRUDE - FUTURE (MAY)
11795.5

LONG BRENT
CRUDE OIL

Figure 26

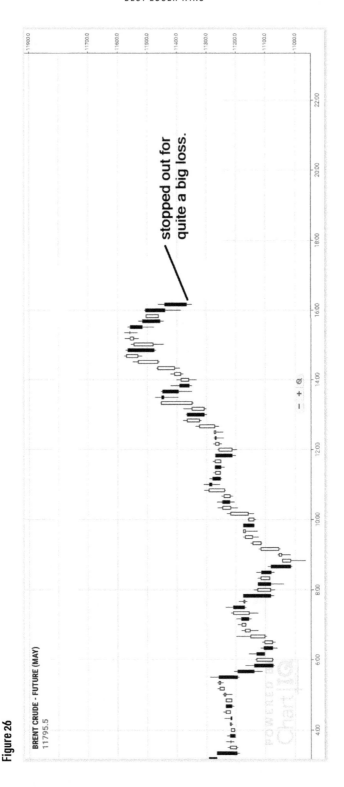

BRENT CRUDE - FUTURE (MAY)
11795.5

stopped out for
quite a big loss.

This is the power of the Book of Truths. I want to remind myself of things like that. I want to remind myself, in the morning, before the trading starts, that Tom Hougaard trades best when he is calm and is not caught up in an emotional whirlpool of excitement and a brain awash with adrenaline and dopamine.

I looked at my trading monitor and saw my position losing me money. I reminded myself that, although I got caught up in the emotions of another trader (one that I respect), I am not him. I am me. I closed the trade, and then I waited. I had made an impulsive trade – an emotional trade without a real plan or a real setup. I wasn't annoyed so much with the losing trade as much as I was annoyed with suddenly being impulsive and acting without truly thinking. I could have spent 30 seconds thinking it through and the outcome would have been very different.

I calmed myself down, and I thoroughly analysed the chart, and I decided upon a better entry point. I used my *process* – the tools that work for me. And then this pattern in Figure 27 showed up. It was late in the day, and I was prepared for a restful evening after a long trading week. I bought Brent, and I held it.

The setup is simply a Harmonic Retracement. The first retracement and the second retracement are identical. It gives razor-sharp entries, where it is easy to control your risk.

I want to remind myself of the things I do well. I want to remind myself of the things I can be prone to when I am not calm. I want to do that ahead of the open. I accept that I will never be perfect. I will at times still make stupid Brent Oil trades on a Friday afternoon because a friend of mine is telling me of his success; but I like to think that like a missile I will self-coordinate as new data becomes apparent, and I like to think that my mental preparation makes my mistakes short lived.

Figure 27

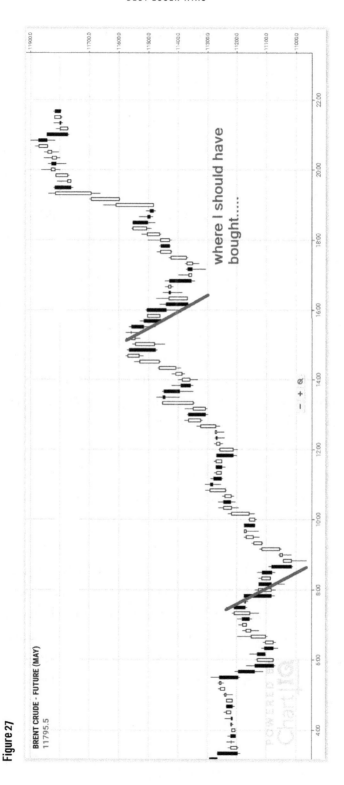

TRUST

My review of my trades revealed that I didn't trust myself or the markets. Profitable trading requires trust. If you don't believe it can happen, you should not even start. If you don't trust, then you will not make money. Therefore, before you start trading again, you have to work on your beliefs about yourself and the markets.

As I see it, trust falls into two categories.

TRUST YOURSELF

You have to trust that you already have all the tools you need to make a living from trading. Yes, you need to acquire a certain competence level in the field of technical analysis (or whatever edge you use to make trading decisions).

I continue to study technical analysis, and I do so to improve my understanding of the ever-changing nature of the markets I trade, but it is not technical analysis that will make me money. It is trusting that I already have all the skills I need to make money consistently.

The reason why I was not more successful in my early trading was not because I didn't know enough about technical analysis. It was because I thought the only thing I needed was technical analysis. However, that was, and is, simply not true.

I had not focused my time and attention on matters outside of technical analysis. My focus was not on the right things. My technical savvy was not matched by an emotional maturity, because I had not spent time working on that side of my game.

You need to trust that you already have all that you need. Otherwise, you will not bridge the gap between what you know you can achieve and what you are achieving. You need to believe. The belief comes from doing. I will address that in a moment.

TRUST MARKETS

The second trust consideration is the trust in the markets. When I go to work in the morning, it would be great if the perfect setup manifested itself before my eyes right at the opening bell. However, it rarely does.

I use a five-minute and a ten-minute chart as my primary trading time frame. A typical trading session runs over ten hours for me. That means I will be confronted with a total of 120 candles/bars of five-minute duration.

As a result of my review of my trading performance, I came to a realisation. I didn't trust the market would give me the opportunities I needed to make money. It was a debilitating belief.

I set out to prove that I was wrong in that belief by reviewing ten years' worth of intra-day data from the handful of products that I traded most frequently. Now I wasn't just studying for the sake of identifying patterns. I studied to prove that the technical analysis setups that served me well would repeat every day.

I arrived at a new set of beliefs. I came to believe I can trust the market to give me an opportunity to make money every day. I came to trust the fact that at least two or three of those five-minute candles would produce a great trade entry.

I came to trust that the market would give me a perfect entry point, such as a double top in a higher time frame downtrend or a continuation signal. In conclusion, I shaped a new belief around the evidence that I laid bare through my research. I came to accept that I can produce a good living from trading, from waiting for those ideal setups.

But those ideal setups don't necessarily materialise when I want them to, in the time frame I have at my disposal to trade. I need something else beyond trust.

Trust is a vital part of the journey to making the markets your playground, but it is not the only component. I needed to work on another part of my behaviour. I would often tire before the afternoon trading session. I would often tire as the week progressed. This led to poor decisions, which can be directly attributed to boredom and impatience.

PATIENCE

I realised that my patience was my weakness. However, there is more than one kind of patience. For example, a mother teaching her young child to read may experience a sense of impatience, but the mother will remind herself that eventually all children learn how to read.

The impatience that a parent may experience is mitigated by the perceived time horizon to reach the end goal. We know our children will learn basic reading skills, as long as we persist. We simply have to maintain our patience as our little ones inch their way towards the desired skill.

You can't argue that patience is a quality directly transferable from parenting to trading. As a parent you can tell yourself you will patiently work towards your child being able to read. However, you can't say that you will patiently wait for the market to hit your desired entry point, because it might *not* hit your desired entry point.

As a result, you will experience emotions that a parent doesn't. You will experience a fear that the market will move without you. You will be fearful that the market will not give you an opportunity to jump on board. Without the right kind of conditioning, you will act upon these fear impulses.

Had I not gone through all the data I had, I would not have been so assured in my decision to wait for the right setup. I accept my process is thorough, but with that preparation comes significant financial reward.

Without a doubt, one of the greatest flaws I saw traders exhibit during my decade on a London trading floor was the idea that it is *too late* to join the trend. It was a common occurrence during trend days to witness clients continuously try to find the low of the day.

On those days our clients lost the most. If the market was rallying, they would either do nothing, or they would try to find a place to sell short. If the market was falling, they would do nothing; but more likely they would try to find the low of the day and buy.

Considering the action was so common across such a large group of individuals, I conclude that there is an inherent trading flaw in our thinking which makes us want to go against the trend. I have previously mentioned this *supermarket mentality*, which compels us to seek *value*.

Another reason this behaviour is commonplace is because of the prolific use of chart indicators that display what is technically known as overbought and oversold price levels. The use of overbought and oversold indicators has a terrible track record in trending markets.

To my mind patience is a skillset that can make the difference between being an abject failure or a wizard. I used the word *skillset* because I believe that patience can be developed.

I developed my patience in trading using two methods. Both are practical in nature, but they are very different in their application. One is a proactive exercise. One is a reflective exercise.

EXPANDING MY FIELD OF INFORMATION

The proactive exercise evolved around the concept of expanding the field of information. I print out the charts of my favourite markets every night, while the trading session is still fresh in my mind. For example, I will print out the DAX Index chart and the FTSE Index chart on both a five-minute chart and a ten-minute chart.

The reason I am printing out two time frames is because of perspective. I found that my use of the five-minute chart prompted overtrading. By considering the ten-minute chart I am forcing myself to slow down my decision making. This act of slowing down my time perspective also strengthens my patience. I see things on a ten-minute chart that give me a greater clarity than if I had seen them on a five-minute chart alone.

Patience, however, is not a quality that is easy to come by. I am a man in my 50s. Over my lifespan the world has pandered to the impatient. When I was a child, if my family ran out of milk on a Sunday afternoon I would have to wait until Monday morning before I could purchase another bottle. Everything was shut on a Sunday.

Forgive me if I sound like a relic. I am really not. I love technological advances. So many wonderful things flow from our advancement of living, but the flipside of the coin is that we as a species have also become impatient.

That is important to remember when you set out on a trading journey. Not long ago, I read about a gentleman called Navinder Sarao, a trader who became synonymous with the infamous 2010 flash crash. In the book *Flash Crash*, by Liam Vaughan, it becomes apparent that some of the primary skills that Navinder possessed were focus and patience. According to the book, Navinder Sarao would hide himself away from the other traders he worked with, so as not to be disturbed. He needed quiet around him to exercise focus and patience.

The exercise of printing out the specific charts every day instils in me faith that every day the market will give me an opportunity to make good trades. The exercise is also an opportunity for me to discover new behaviour in the market and continuously train my mind and eyes to spot patterns. I happen to believe that you only see things you have trained your eyes to see.

IMAGERY AND BREATHING

The second exercise is hard to begin with. Some call this exercise meditation. Some call it visual imagery. I don't have a name for it, but I know what I want to achieve. I want to calm down my mind. Depending on the mood I am in, I will use one of the following tools to keep my mind trained for the task of being a high-stake day trader.

I sit quietly in a comfortable position, and I observe my breath. I breathe in for seven seconds, and I breathe out for 11. I repeat. I will do as much or as little as I need to feel calm coming over me. Sometimes it takes five minutes. Sometimes it takes 15 minutes.

The purpose of the exercise is simply to calm my mind. Through the use of breathing exercises I have been able to increase my attention span significantly. I was hesitant at first. I was even hesitant to write about it. It has that taste of a new-age fad. The reality is that calming your mind through breathwork is used extensively by high-performance athletes. I read extensively on the topic of meditation amongst Formula 1 drivers. It was both a surprise and a relief that ultra-competitive sportsmen and women, people I admire and am inspired by, are turning their sight inwards to improve their edge.

I have to be upfront with you. I have no formal training in meditation or imagery. I simply trust and let myself be guided by what enters my head. My mental imagery is designed to place myself in physically dangerous situations. I may be face to face with an alligator. I may climb a steep rock face. I may surf a monstrous swell. The exercise is simple. I want to elevate my pulse through imagery. Then I want to consciously focus on my breath and simply accept the situation for what it is. The aim is to confront the imagery and remain calm.

Once I am calm, I see myself trading the absolute biggest stake size I am allowed by my broker. I see the market move against me, and I visualise my P&L go deeply into negative. I feel my pulse elevate, and I focus on calming it down. I repeat this process over and over.

I see myself riding a trend higher and higher. I see my P&L grow larger and larger. I am waiting for my mind to tell me to take profit. Then I *stop the tape and flip the switch*. I calm my mind down, and I see myself looking at my P&L dispassionately. I calm my breath until I am able to simply observe my profit grow larger and larger as I trend with the market, higher and higher. The goal is simply to *be*, to be an unemotional observer of the market. The goal is to act without fear, without hope, without anything but an objective assessment of the price action.

ASK FOR HELP

I believe that beliefs shape our lives. I believe not all my beliefs are beneficial to the life I want to live. I accept they are there, and as my self-knowledge evolves I address them to the best of my ability. I have come up with this back-to-front idea of how to address my beliefs.

It evolves around the old saying, "I will believe it when I see it." How about turning it on its head to say, "I will see it when I believe it"? This argues that you must *believe* before you can *see*. Many of our beliefs have been part of our construct since our formative years. They are not going to go away without a fight. Of course you might decide not to fight them, but to accept them.

I call this process *Ask for Help*. I sit with a blank piece of paper, and I pose a question. It could be, "Why am I afraid to join a down-trend after it already started?" I write down everything that appears in my mind. I sit with my eyes closed and I observe my thoughts. I do not censor myself. I just sit and ask and listen and write down.

I may write for 10–20 minutes. What often appears on paper are thoughts straight out of the psych ward. It scares me at times how brutally to the point and honest the answers can be. It can be quite horrifying to read the things the subconscious mind brings up. I don't judge. I accept.

When I am working with my beliefs, fighting those beliefs will not work. I think giving negative energy to a belief will only cause it to fight for its life. The only thing that works is complete acceptance. I accept what is there. I understand it. It allows me to retire it. I diffuse it. If I approach it from a perspective of "I hate this belief", it will enforce and entrench itself.

Say I have a belief about trading that suggests I need to make my money quickly. I need to get in on the move first thing in the morning. If I want to diffuse this belief, because I have strong evidence to suggest it is destructive to my trading account, I will ask for help. I will accept the belief. I will diffuse its negative energy, and I will replace it with positive energy. I will reinforce a new belief such as "I will wait for the first ten-minute bar to complete before I make a decision to trade".

Unfortunately, beliefs do not have the power to dismantle themselves. All beliefs demand expression. Desire and willingness to ask questions from a sincere space, with a sincere mindset, will give you answers.

When I use the Ask for Help process, I know it is complete when I can distil my question into a short one-sentence answer. Then I know I have condensed the exercise into its lowest common denominator, and I have diffused whatever belief I had that didn't serve me. The old memory will always be there, but the context has changed from negative to positive.

It is important for me to remind you that money is a by-product of the ideal trading mindset. You are creating a process that will guarantee an optimal mindset for your trading life. The essence of good trading lies squarely in how we think and perceive information about the markets. It has everything to do with how we think and how we live our lives.

Today I spoke to a friend of mine. We had not spoken in a while. I consider him a very close friend, and it was a joy to reconnect. As he spoke, I listened intently. You have two ears and one mouth. Use them in that proportion. He was talking animatedly about his trading and how well it was going. In between the stream of sentences, I picked up on a sentence that spoke volumes: "I am still working on increasing my trading size."

I thought long and hard about that sentence, knowing I was going to write this final chapter today. My friend first spoke to me about increasing his trading size back in 2015. Today it is 2022. He has spent seven years talking about increasing his trading size. What does that tell you about his desire to increase his trading size? Do you think there might be a misalignment between what he says he wants, and what he is actually doing to get what he wants?

I often tell my children this. Do what you have to do, so that you can do what you want to do. I tell them to make up their minds what they want but think very long and hard about it first. If you say you want something, and then you do nothing about it, then you can be damn certain there is a misalignment between your conscious and your subconscious. When I am faced with a situation like that, I use the Ask for Help exercise, and I always get a brutally honest answer. The most common answer I get is: "Actually you say want it, but you don't!"

The idea of deciding what you want can undo a lifetime of negative energy surrounding your beliefs and your belief system. The power of making up your mind will remove all negative energy surrounding a belief system. I have come to accept that many people do not want to do that. We fall in love with our drama. We cling on to our drama because it validates us and gives us attention.

When I am out of sorts, angry, frustrated, I ask questions and work my way backwards. I work my way to the source of the problem. Anger is often a self-defence mechanism. If I am angry, I need to know what the underlying belief for the anger is. So, I ask.

I am often told I am very disciplined. This is not true. The word itself is an oxymoron. Discipline implies the use of force and will. My action flows from a love of what I do. I don't have to apply will to do what I do. Those who are self-disciplined don't think of themselves as self-disciplined. They are just expressing themselves in harmony with their own dreams and goals and desires.

When you watch spiritual movies like *The Secret* and listen to self-help tapes, you get this sense that the universe is a menu, and you can help yourself to whatever you want. I find that to be one of the most distressing aspects of the self-help industry, be it neurolinguistic programming or Law of Attraction or whatever name the latest fad goes by.

I have stood in an auditorium and listened to motivational speakers make their audience shout out whatever grievances are holding them back, and then push the audience towards their private island retreat for untold sums. I never believed in it. I don't believe anyone ever achieved anything spectacular without putting in a massive amount of effort. I know I put in the effort. I know that everything I do on a daily basis is the result of grit and determination. I am not talented. I am hard working. I am not gifted. I am determined. I am not lucky. I am persistent.

TWENTY TRADES

My friend Dr David Paul gave me an exercise, which at its heart is designed to strengthen the process of your trading. It is as simple as it is difficult. Your job is to execute 20 trades, as the signals appear.

One by one, you take every trade signal as it comes. The purpose of the exercise is not actually to make money. You will probably break even, and that is fine. The purpose of the exercise is to *smoke out* your internal conflicts and your unresolved emotions.

It has at its core the idea that if you can execute 20 trades without any kind of conflict, you are trading from a carefree and fearless frame of mind. This means you are trading from the perspective that:

1. Anything can happen – and you are emotionally detached from the outcome.

2. Every moment is unique – and you are no longer drawing associations between this moment and another moment. You are pain free.

3. There is a random distribution of wins and losses – you accept the outcome as if it were a coin-flip exercise.

4. You don't have to know what will happen next to make money – so you trust the process, and you focus on controlling the only variable you truly can control, which is how much you want to risk on this trade.

The purpose of the exercise is to add energy to your beliefs. Until you can do that without conflict and unresolved thoughts and conflicting energy issues, the negative charge will not dissipate.

How do you know when you are successful? When you can trade without any conflicting or competing thoughts. The results are not important during the exercise. This a process exercise. You may have to repeat the 20 trades over and over until you come to a point where you find that you are firing off trades without fear, without hesitation, without connecting this moment with a past moment, and you accept the outcome dispassionately. When you arrive there, you really have arrived!

DISASSOCIATION

A friend called. She had put up a post on a social media outlet, and her post was very ill received. She endured a torrent of abuse for what was a well-intentioned post. She called me for help. I read her post and the slew of abusive comments. To me, however, they were just words. They were words without energy.

I dispassionately read the posts, and then I explained to her what to do. As traders we need to work towards being as dispassionate about our trading as I was about her social media post. The more we work on this, the better we will trade. Some will argue against me. Remember, I am writing this from the perspective of what works for me.

How do you do trade dispassionately? How do you disassociate yourself from feeling anything when you are trading? Well, that is what my exercises take care of. If you want to be able to receive information from the market, without feeling threatened, it will not happen by itself. I believe working on *what you think* and *how you respond and evaluate your responses* will improve your trading in measures you would struggle to appreciate right now.

I once sped down the *autobahn* doing 186 miles an hour. Yes, it was reckless. Whilst doing it, I wasn't wondering if there was milk in the fridge or if I had remembered to floss my teeth this morning. I was in the moment. Focused. That is what I want to bring to my trading every day.

Every moment is unique. That does not mean we have to act like a formless blob with no memory of the past. There will always be some degree of correspondence. However, just because I was rejected by a girl the first time I invited her for a dance does not mean I will be rejected the next time. But my mind might think so, so I may have an argument with my conscious thinking and my subconscious beliefs.

My rational mind might say, "The next girl will say yes to a dance." My subconscious mind, unbeknownst to me, might say, "No way amigo, give up, she will never dance with you." If you have a moment of doubt before venturing over to ask the lucky lady, you know you are not aligned. When I experience this in my trading, I will Ask for Help, or I will use imagery to resolve whatever is going on in my head.

MIND LOOP

My training involves accepting pain and making it part of my existence through habit and repetition, so that my degree of pain tolerance is expanded. I also have to train my mind about expectations, and how to deal with unrealised expectations.

This requires a tenacious effort, through journalling, mental imagery, and asking for help. You may quite rightly ask, "Does it work?" I think it does. It has revolutionised my trading. As I type these words, in March 2022, I have not had a losing day since September 2021. That is nearly seven months without a single losing day.

I don't think this should be celebrated. I am not writing this to show off in any shape or form. The intention is to inspire you to take the mental side of trading almost as seriously as the technical side. If I were to describe the beliefs that are the foundation for my trading, they would resemble a flowchart, one where the entire mindset ecosystem forms a loop.

My trust (in the markets and in myself) supports my patience. My patience (that a setup will materialise) feeds my confidence. My confidence (that I will win) dictates my inner dialogue. My inner dialogue (what I tell myself while I am trading) supports my process-oriented mindset. The process enables me to stay focused in this moment. I support this loop with my mental exercises. They feed, nourish and sustain the loop.

I am a process-oriented trader. I do not believe in goal setting. There are no Post-It Notes on my monitor reminding me how much I want to make today or this month or year. I have no monetary goals or pip/point goals. I will take what the market will give me. I *never* trade with targets.

By being utterly focused on the process as opposed to being outcome oriented, I ensure that I am staying *present*. When you are present, you don't connect past moments with this moment or future moments. You are right here, right now.

Being present is what some would call mindfulness. I call it focus. I call it concentration. I call it *knowing what I want*. I want to win. That is my overriding motive for trading – to win. I want to win, but I don't mind losing.

However, I know that if I forget all about winning, and I focus on the process, I will win. It is an idiosyncratic conundrum that for a long time I just could not believe and give into. How can I win if I am not focused on the goal at all times?

It took me almost a decade to figure out that *process is everything*. Don't focus on the goal. Sure, know what the goal is, but focus on the process. Trust the process. I built my trading life around this mind loop. How does the loop look?

I trust. The research underpins the trust. The trust supports the patience. The patience is underpinned by the mental exercises, and it nourishes my confidence. My internal dialogue is driven by a process-oriented mindset, fuelled by my confidence. I focus on what I can control – my mindset, my risk approach – and I let the market do what it wants to do. Whatever it does, does not fuel the fearful side of my mind. That has been trained away. I am not afraid of the market. The only thing I am afraid of is that I do something stupid in the market. As I trust myself, this does not happen.

I trust that I have the skills to make money, and I trust that the market will give me opportunities to make money. This trust has been nurtured and strengthened by my intense study of market charts for the time period I desire to trade. The trust is further strengthened by continuous dedication to my vocational skillset.

My patience flows from my trust in the market and in myself. I have built an emotional connection between trust and patience. I trust the setups will come, if I am patient. If I am patient, I will win. Winning means more than anything else to me. If I am not patient, I will not win. I will do anything to win. Therefore, the trust overrides any emotional impatience that may arise in my mind, because I trust that if I miss this signal, there will be another one coming.

My confidence comes from continuously working on my game. I don't learn technical analysis once. I learn all the time. Some markets move. Some markets are dead. Some markets require larger stops. Some require you to trade with orders because they move so fast. The markets are forever changing, and I change with them.

My inner dialogue stems from the trust and the patience and the confidence. Of course, *yours truly* has bad trading days. I just don't let it bother me. I am grounded in this moment. I focus on the process. That is all I can do. I can't dictate to the market what it must do. I must be like water, and *flow*. I must flow with the market. I don't fight the market. I flow with the market. "Just flow," I tell myself.

This is what lies behind the process. I never expect to be comfortable when I am trading. If I am comfortable, I know I am not pushing the boundaries of what I am capable of. I know that to get the best out of myself I need to be a little uncomfortable. I will give you an example.

I sold short the Dow Index in my Telegram channel (timestamped for authenticity and verification). I have marked my entry point in Figure 28. Initially, the market moves against me. Then it turns and trends lower. As it trends lower, I am mindful of my mind saying, "Take profit." That voice used to be much louder. Now I am so focused on the process that the voice is no longer heard. I focus on the process, not on the outcome.

However, at one point I have 200 points in profit and the market sits at an old low. I have to accept that there is a real possibility the market will rebound from there, and much of my 200-point profit will disappear. *That* is being uncomfortable. I accept it and decide to let the position ride.

Do you know why I let it ride? Because I know myself well enough to accept that if I took profit, and the market then continued lower, I would feel awful. The pain of seeing a market giving you even more profit when you are not on board is much greater than the pain of seeing some of your paper profit disappear – to me at least!

This time it worked. Tomorrow it might not work. I have to trust the process will sustain me over the long run and be less concerned about the outcome of a single event. Remember, there is complete randomness in the outcome of one event, but over hundreds of observations there is no randomness.

A trading life is not defined by what we do every now and then, but by what we do over and over. You will never be able to trade without having losing trades. The whole purpose for giving this book the title it has, *Best Loser Wins*, is to illustrate this point right from

Figure 28

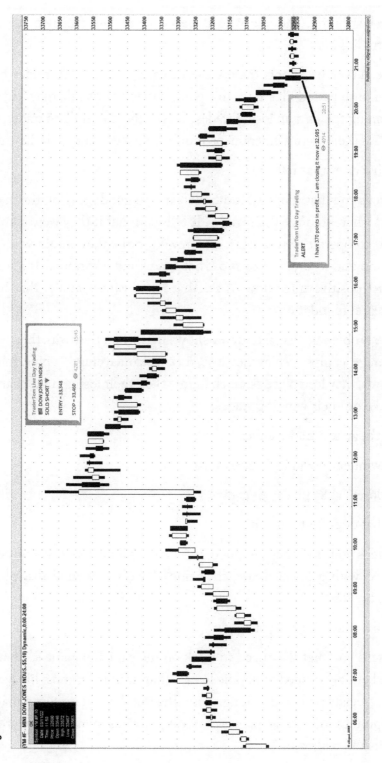

the beginning. The one who is best able to lose will win the game of trading.

The survey of 25,000 traders executing 43 million FX trades over a 15-month period illustrates this point perfectly. Overall, they had more winning trades than losing trades. Out of those 43 million trades, up to 61% of them were winners, depending on what currency pair they traded.

What does that tell you?

It tells you that those 25,000 traders have a good grasp on the markets and where to place their trades. It tells you that if they were somehow able to operate with a 1:1 risk-to-reward ratio, they would win 61 out of 100 and lose 39 out of 100. That is a winning formula. That creates a net positive trade flow of 22. That is a business model that has an integral foundation.

The problem is that the survey shows that when they win, they win on average 43 pips. When they lose, they lose on average 83 pips. In other words, they lose twice as much (almost) on their losing trade than they make on their winning trades.

Let's say 100 trades are executed.

61 winners at 43 pips = 2,623 pips

39 losers at 83 pips = 3,237 pips

What does that tell you?

It tells you that they are good at picking winners, but when they are faced with a losing trade, they don't have the mental discipline to cut the loss.

What does *that* tell you?

It tells you that they need to work on their mental game so that they are better equipped to handle losses. Their minds are most likely wired to associate pain with taking a loss. The mind has at its core a mandate to protect you against pain – physical as well as mental pain, perceived pain and real pain.

FINAL WORDS

Your path to becoming a profitable trader lies not in better understanding the markets, but in better understanding your mind. Your mind and how you operate it will dictate the level of success you have as a trader.

I am going to go out on a limb and tell you something about *you*. People reading this book could have fallen into one of two categories, but I doubt it. I doubt that new traders, who have never traded before, will ever gravitate towards a book like mine.

They are more likely to buy books that have titles like *Mastering Trading* or *Trade Your Way to Financial Independence*. This kind of book will be 300 pages of technical analysis and most likely not contain a single mention of losing trades. It will contain page after page of perfect chart examples.

This book, I speculate, will be read by the people who previously bought the sort of book mentioned above, but have come to the realisation that the gap between where they are now and where they know they can be can only be bridged by a better mindset.

The advantage I have in writing this book is that I don't have to establish my credentials. I have a four-year public track record, timestamped and readily available for anyone to read. I post my broker trades in Excel format on my website and in my Telegram channel daily. There are plenty of bad trades in that track record, I assure you, but somehow I still manage to make money overall, and quite significantly so.

Therefore, the focus now needs to be on the actual steps I have taken – and still take – to ensure I stay at the top of my game. That is where you are headed now.

I want to finish the book on a note which is important to me. I have described a process that works for me. It is based around my particular beliefs. Those beliefs are the result of my particular life circumstances.

I believe that beliefs are defined by one's own desires and needs. As a result of my desire to be a profitable trader, and my need to create financial stability in my life, I have acquired beliefs that are consistent with this goal.

That said, I accept that my way is not the only way. I don't describe *the* way. I describe *my* way. Whatever you decide is right for you is right for you. Trust it.

I periodically suffer from verbal diarrhoea on the mental aspect of trading. I post my musings on both www.BestLoserWins.com as well as on my website www.TraderTom.com

Have a wonderful journey.

With love.

Tom Hougaard

ABOUT THE AUTHOR

TOM HOUGAARD studied economics and finance at two universities in the United Kingdom, and then went on to work for JPMorgan Chase before spending the next ten years in the City of London as a chief market strategist for a CFD broker. He has given thousands of TV and radio interviews on the state of the market and has educated tens of thousands of clients on trading strategies. Since 2009 he has traded for himself.

Tom has self-published several works on trading psychology, price action and product knowledge.

You can follow Tom's trading via Telegram and YouTube. You can view his trading results at www.tradertom.com